GW01237171

95

SPECIAL NEEDS IN ORDINARY
General Editor: Peter Mittler

Shut Up! Communication in the Secondary
School

Special Needs in Ordinary Schools

General editor: Peter Mittler
Associate editors: James Hogg, Peter Pumfrey, Tessa Roberts, Colin Robson
Honorary advisory board: Neville Bennett, Marion Blythman, George Cooke, John Fish, Ken Jones, Sylvia Phillips, Klaus Wedell, Phillip Williams

Titles in this series

Shut Up!
Communication in the
Secondary School

Bernadette Walsh

Cassell

For my pupils

Cassell Educational Limited:
Artillery House
Artillery Row
London SW1P 1RT

First published 1988

British Library Cataloguing in Publication Data
Walsh, Bernadette
  Shut up!: communication in the secondary
  school.—(Special needs in ordinary
  schools).
  1. Secondary schools. Learning disordered
  students. Communication skills. Development
  I. Title II. Series
  371.9'044

ISBN: 0 – 304 – 31454 – 4

Phototypesetting by Activity Ltd., Salisbury, Wiltshire
Printed and bound in Great Britain by Biddles Ltd.,
Guildford and King's Lynn.

Last digit is print no: 9 8 7 6 5 4 3 2 1

Contents

Acknowledgements

Throughout the writing of this book, Peter Pumfrey has been my facilitator. For his advice and detailed editorial comments, I offer my sincere thanks. I express my gratitude also to Ian McMillan for his permission to re-print the poem that amused me.

The writing of one's first book is a good excuse to pay additional tribute to those special people who have helped along the way. I will always be indebted to Bernard Harrison who has been my constant support and guide throughout my post-graduate career.

It was my former Head of Department, Eileen Tomlinson, who first trusted me to teach children with special needs. I can never thank her enough for her continuing friendship.

Thanks are also due to Moyra Bentley, Eddie and Rowena Errington and especially Annily Campbell for her tolerance, all of whom shared their time and space with me as friends and former colleagues at Scarborough.

I am also grateful to Maureen Stevenson, Mary Magill and Deborah Skelton for their support and for the interest they have shown in my work, not least because they know the difficulties of teaching those with special needs.

I thank Carol Wilson for her typing in the early stages and my sister, Philomena, for later word-processing.

Ironically, those who most deserve my gratitude will probably never read this, namely the pupils I taught, whose special needs made this book possible.

Foreword: Towards education for all

AIMS

This series aims to support teachers as they respond to the challenge they face in meeting the needs of all children in their school, particularly those identified as having special educational needs.

Although there have been many useful publications in the field of special educational needs during the last decade, the distinguishing feature of the present series of volumes lies in their concern with specific areas of the curriculum in primary and secondary schools. We have tried to produce a series of conceptually coherent and professionally relevant books, each of which is concerned with ways in which children with varying levels of ability and motivation can be taught together. The books draw on the experience of practising teachers, teacher trainers and researchers and seek to provide practical guidelines on ways in which specific areas of the curriculum can be made more accessible to all children. The volumes provide many examples of curriculum adaptation, classroom activities, teacher–child interactions, as well as the mobilisation of resources inside and outside the school.

The series is organised largely in terms of age and subject groupings, but three 'overview' volumes have been prepared in order to provide an account of some major current issues and developments. Seamus Hegarty's *Meeting Special Needs in Ordinary Schools* gives an introduction to the field of special needs as a whole, whilst Sheila Wolfendale's *Primary Schools and Special Needs* and John Sayer's *Secondary Schools for All?* address issues more specifically concerned with primary and secondary schools respectively. We hope that curriculum specialists will find essential background and contextual material in these overview volumes.

In addition, a section of this series will be concerned with examples of obstacles to learning. All of these specific special needs can be seen on a continuum ranging from mild to severe, or from temporary and transient to long-standing or permanent. These include difficulties in learning or in adjustment and behaviour, as well as problems resulting largely from sensory or physical impairments or from difficulties of communication from whatever cause. We hope that teachers will consult the volumes in this section for guidance on working with children with specific difficulties.

The series aims to make a modest 'distance learning' contribution to meeting the needs of teachers working with the whole range of pupils with special educational needs by offering a set of resource materials relating to specific areas of the primary and secondary curriculum and by suggesting ways in which learning obstacles, whatever their origin, can be identified and addressed.

We hope that these materials will not only be used for private study but be subjected to critical scrutiny by school-based inservice groups sharing common curricular interests and by staff of institutions of higher education concerned with both special needs teaching and specific curriculum areas. The series has been planned to provide a resource for Local Education Authority (LEA) advisers, specialist teachers from all sectors of the education service, educational psychologists, and teacher working parties. We hope that the books will provide a stimulus for dialogue and serve as catalysts for improved practice.

It is our hope that parents will also be encouraged to read about new ideas in teaching children with special needs so that they can be in a better position to work in partnership with teachers on the basis of an informed and critical understanding of current difficulties and developments. The goal of 'Education for All' can only be reached if we succeed in developing a working partnership between teachers, pupils, parents, and the community at large.

ELEMENTS OF A WHOLE-SCHOOL APPROACH

Meeting special educational needs in ordinary schools is much more than a process of opening school doors to admit children previously placed in special schools. It involves a radical re-examination of what all schools have to offer all children. Our efforts will be judged in the long term by our success with children who are already in ordinary schools but whose needs are not being met, for whatever reason.

The additional challenge of achieving full educational as well as social integration for children now in special schools needs to be seen in the wider context of a major reappraisal of what ordinary schools have to offer the pupils already in them. The debate about integration of handicapped and disabled children in ordinary schools should not be allowed to overshadow the movement for curriculum reform in the schools themselves. If successful, this could promote the fuller integration of the children already in the schools.

If this is the aim of current policy, as it is of this series of unit texts, we have to begin by examining ways in which schools and school policies can themselves be a major element in children's difficulties.

Can schools cause special needs?

Traditionally, we have looked for causes of learning difficulty in the child. Children have been subjected to tests and investigations by doctors, psychologists and teachers with the aim of pinpointing the nature of the problem and in the hope that this might lead to specific programmes of teaching and intervention. We less frequently ask ourselves whether what and how we teach and the way in which we organise and manage our schools could themselves be a major cause of children's difficulties.

The shift of emphasis towards a whole-school policy is sometimes described in terms of a move away from the deficit or medical model of special education towards a more environmental or ecological model. Clearly, we are concerned here with an interaction between the two. No one would deny that the origins of some learning difficulties do lie in the child. But even where a clear cause can be established — for example, a child with severe brain damage, or one with a serious sensory or motor disorder — it would be simplistic to attribute all the child's learning difficulties to the basic impairment alone.

The ecological model starts from the position that the growth and development of children can be understood only in relation to the nature of their interactions with the various environments which impinge on them and with which they are constantly interacting. These environments include the home and each individual member of the immediate and extended family. Equally important are other children in the neighbourhood and at school, as well as people with whom the child comes into casual or closer contact. We also need to consider the local and wider community and its various institutions — not least, the powerful influence of television, which for some children represents more hours of information intake than is provided by teachers during eleven years of compulsory education. The ecological model thus describes a gradually widening series of concentric circles, each of which provides a powerful series of influences and possibilities for interaction — and therefore learning.

Schools and schooling are only one of many environmental influences affecting the development and learning of children. A great deal has been learned from other environments before the child enters school and much more will be learned after the child leaves full-time education. Schools represent a relatively powerful series of environments, not all concerned with formal learning. During the hours spent in school, it is hard to estimate the extent to which the number and nature of the interactions experienced by any one child are directly concerned with formal teaching and learning. Social interactions with other children also need to be considered.

Questions concerned with access to the curriculum lie at the heart of any whole-school policy. What factors limit the access of certain children to the curriculum? What modifications are necessary to ensure fuller curriculum access? Are there areas of the curriculum from which some children are excluded? Is this because they are thought 'unlikely to be able to benefit'? And even if they are physically present, are there particular lessons or activities which are inaccessible because textbooks or worksheets demand a level of literacy and comprehension which effectively prevent access? Are there tasks in which children partly or wholly fail to understand the language which the teacher is using? Are some teaching styles inappropriate for individual children?

Is it possible that some learning difficulties arise from the ways in which schools are organised and managed? For example, what messages are we conveying when we separate some children from others? How does the language we use to describe certain children reflect our own values and assumptions? How do schools transmit value judgements about children who succeed and those who do not? In the days when there was talk of comprehensive schools being 'grammar schools for all', what hope was there for children who were experiencing significant learning difficulties? And even today, what messages are we transmitting to children and their peers when we exclude them from participation in some school activities? How many children with special needs will be entered for the new General Certificate of Secondary Education (GCSE) examinations? How many have taken or will take part in Technical and Vocational Education Initiative (TVEI) schemes?

The argument here is not that all children should have access to all aspects of the curriculum. Rather it is a plea for the individualisation of learning opportunities for all children. This requires a broad curriculum with a rich choice of learning opportunities designed to suit the very wide range of individual needs.

Curriculum reform

The last decade has seen an increasingly interventionist approach by Her Majesty's Inspectors of Education (HMI), by officials of the Department of Education and Science (DES) and by individual Secretaries of State. The 'Great Debate', allegedly beginning in 1976, led to a flood of curriculum guidelines from the centre. The garden is secret no longer. Whilst Britain is far from the centrally imposed curriculum found in some other countries, government is increasingly insisting that schools must reflect certain key areas of experience for all pupils, and in particular those concerned with the world of work (*sic*), with science and technology, and with economic awareness. These priorities are also reflected in the prescriptions for teacher education laid down with an increasing degree of firmness from the centre.

There are indications that a major reappraisal of curriculum content and access is already under way and seems to be well supported by teachers. Perhaps the best known and most recent examples can be found in the series of Inner London Education Authority (ILEA) reports concerned with secondary, primary and special education, known as the Hargreaves, Thomas and Fish Reports (ILEA, 1984, 1985a, 1985b). In particular, the Hargreaves Report envisaged a radical reform of the secondary curriculum, based to some extent on his book *Challenge for the Comprehensive School* (Hargreaves, 1982). This envisages a major shift of emphasis from the 'cognitive–academic' curriculum of many secondary schools towards one emphasising more personal involvement by pupils in selecting their own patterns of study from a wider range of choice. If the proposals in these reports were to be even partially implemented, pupils with special needs would stand to benefit from such a wholesale review of the curriculum of the school as a whole.

Pupils with special needs also stand to benefit from other developments in mainstream education. These include new approaches to records of achievement, particularly 'profiling' and a greater emphasis on criterion-referenced assessment. Some caution has already been expressed about the extent to which the new GCSE examinations will reach less able children previously excluded from the Certificate of Secondary Education. Similar caution is justified in relation to the TVEI and the Certificate of Pre-Vocational Education (CPVE). And what about the new training initiatives for school leavers and the 14–19 age group in general? Certainly, the pronouncements of the Manpower Services Commission (MSC) emphasise a policy of provision for all, and have made specific arrangements for young people with special needs, including those with disabilities. In the last analysis, society and its institutions will be judged by their success in preparing the majority of young people to make an effective and valued contribution to the community as a whole.

A CLIMATE OF CHANGE

Despite the very real and sometimes overwhelming difficulties faced by schools and teachers as a result of underfunding and professional unrest, there are encouraging signs of change and reform which, if successful, could have a significant impact not only

on children with special needs but on all children. Some of these are
briefly mentioned below.

The campaign for equal opportunities

First, we are more aware of the need to confront issues concerned
with civil rights and equal opportunities. All professionals concerned with human services are being asked to examine their
own attitudes and practices and to question the extent to which
these might unwittingly or even deliberately discriminate unfairly
against some sections of the population.

We are more conscious than ever of the need to take positive steps
to promote the full access of girls and women not only to full
educational opportunities but also to the whole range of community
resources and services, including employment, leisure, housing,
social security and the right to property. We have a similar concern
for members of ethnic and religious groups who have been and still
are victims of discrimination and restricted opportunities for
participation in society and its institutions. It is no accident that the
title of the Swann Report on children from ethnic minorities was
Education for All (Committee of Inquiry, 1985). This too is the theme
of the present series and the underlying aim of the movement to
meet the whole range of special needs in ordinary schools.

The equal opportunities movement has not itself always fully
accepted people with disabilities and special needs. At national
level, there is no legislation specifically concerned with discrimination against people with disabilities, though this does exist in some
other countries. The Equal Opportunities Commission does not
concern itself with disability issues. On the other hand, an
increasing number of local authorities and large corporations claim
to be 'Equal Opportunities Employers', specifically mentioning
disability alongside gender, ethnicity and sexual orientation.
Furthermore, the 1986 Disabled Persons Act, arising from a private
member's Bill and now on the statute book, seeks to carry forward
for adults some of the more positive features of the 1981 Education
Act — for example, it provides for the rights of all people with
disabilities to take part or be represented in discussion and
decision-making concerning services provided for them.

These developments, however, have been largely concerned with
children or adults with disabilities, rather than with children
already in ordinary schools. Powerful voluntary organisations such
as MENCAP (the Royal Society for Mentally Handicapped Children
and Adults) and the Spastics Society have helped to raise political
and public awareness of the needs of children with disabilities and
have fought hard and on the whole successfully to secure better

services for them and for their families. Similarly, organisations of adults with disabilities, such as the British Council of Organisations for Disabled People, are pressing hard for better quality, integrated education, given their own personal experiences of segregated provision.

Special needs and social disadvantage

Even these developments have largely bypassed two of the largest groups now in special schools: those with moderate learning difficulties and those with emotional and behavioural difficulties. There are no powerful pressure groups to speak for them, for the same reason that no pressure groups speak for the needs of children with special needs already in ordinary schools. Many of these children come from families which do not readily form themselves into associations and pressure groups. Many of their parents are unemployed, on low incomes or dependent on social security; many live in overcrowded conditions in poor quality housing or have long-standing health problems. Some members of these families have themselves experienced school failure and rejection as children.

Problems of poverty and disadvantage are common in families of children with special needs already in ordinary schools. Low achievement and social disadvantage are clearly associated, though it is important not to assume that there is a simple relation between them. Although most children from socially disadvantaged backgrounds have not been identified as low achieving, there is still a high correlation between social-class membership and educational achievement, with middle-class children distancing themselves increasingly in educational achievements and perhaps also socially from children from working-class backgrounds — another form of segregation within what purports to be the mainstream.

The probability of socially disadvantaged children being identified as having special needs is very much greater than in other children. An early estimate suggested that it was more than seven times as high, when social disadvantage was defined by the presence of all three of the following indices: overcrowding (more than 1.5 persons per room), low income (supplementary benefit or free school meals) and adverse family circumstances (coming from a single-parent home or a home with more than five children) (Wedge and Prosser, 1973). Since this study was published, the number of families coming into these categories has greatly increased as a result of deteriorating economic conditions and changing social circumstances.

In this wider sense, the problem of special needs is largely a problem of social disadvantage and poverty. Children with special needs are therefore doubly vulnerable to underestimation of their abilities: first, because of their family and social backgrounds, and second, because of their low achievements. A recent large-scale study of special needs provision in junior schools suggests that while teachers' attitudes to low-achieving children are broadly positive, they are pessimistic about the ability of such children to derive much benefit from increased special needs provision (Croll and Moses, 1985).

Partnership with parents

The Croll and Moses survey of junior school practice confirms that teachers still tend to attribute many children's difficulties to adverse home circumstances. How many times have we heard comments along the lines of 'What can you expect from a child from that kind of family?' Is this not a form of stereotyping at least as damaging as racist and sexist attitudes?

Partnership with parents of socially disadvantaged children thus presents a very different challenge from that portrayed in the many reports of successful practice in some special schools. Nevertheless, the challenge can be and is being met. Paul Widlake's recent books (1984, 1985) give the lie to the oft-expressed view that some parents are 'not interested in their child's education'. Widlake documents project after project in which teachers and parents have worked well together. Many of these projects have involved teachers visiting homes rather than parents attending school meetings. There is also now ample research to show that children whose parents listen to them reading at home tend to read better and to enjoy reading more than other children (Topping and Wolfendale, 1985; see also Sheila Wolfendale's *Primary Schools and Special Needs*, in the present series).

Support in the classroom

If teachers in ordinary schools are to identify and meet the whole range of special needs, including those of children currently in special schools, they are entitled to support. Above all, this must come from the head teacher and from the senior staff of the school; from any special needs specialists or teams already in the school; from members of the new advisory and support services, as well as from educational psychologists, social workers and any health professionals who may be involved.

This support can take many forms. In the past, support meant removing the child for considerable periods of time into the care of remedial teachers either within the school or coming from outside. Withdrawal now tends to be discouraged, partly because it is thought to be another form of segregation within the ordinary school, and therefore in danger of isolating and stigmatising children, and partly because it deprives children of access to lessons and activities available to other children. In a major survey of special needs provision in middle and secondary schools, Clunies-Ross and Wimhurst (1983) showed that children with special needs were most often withdrawn from science and modern languages in order to find the time to give them extra help with literacy.

Many schools and LEAs are exploring ways in which both teachers and children can be supported without withdrawing children from ordinary classes. For example, special needs teachers increasingly are working alongside their colleagues in ordinary classrooms, not just with a small group of children with special needs but also with all children. Others are working as consultants to their colleagues in discussing the level of difficulty demanded of children following a particular course or specific lesson. An account of recent developments in consultancy is given in Hanko (1985), with particular reference to children with difficulties of behaviour or adjustment.

Although traditional remedial education is undergoing radical reform, major problems remain. Implementation of new approaches is uneven both between and within LEAs. Many schools still have a remedial department or are visited by peripatetic remedial teachers who withdraw children for extra tuition in reading with little time for consultation with school staff. Withdrawal is still the preferred mode of providing extra help in primary schools, as suggested in surveys of current practice (Clunies-Ross and Wimhurst, 1983; Hodgson, Clunies-Ross and Hegarty, 1984; Croll and Moses, 1985).

Nevertheless, an increasing number of schools now see withdrawal as only one of a widening range of options, only to be used where the child's individually assessed needs suggest that this is indeed the most appropriate form of provision. Other alternatives are now being considered. The overall aim of most of these involves the development of a working partnership between the ordinary class teacher and members of teams with particular responsibility for meeting special needs. This partnership can take a variety of forms, depending on particular circumstances and individual preferences. Much depends on the sheer credibility of special needs teachers, their perceived capacity to offer support and advice and, where necessary, direct, practical help.

We can think of the presence of the specialist teacher as being on a continuum of visibility. A 'high-profile' specialist may sit alongside a pupil with special needs, providing direct assistance and support in participating in activities being followed by the rest of the class. A 'low-profile' specialist may join with a colleague in what is in effect a team-teaching situation, perhaps spending a little more time with individuals or groups with special needs. An even lower profile is provided by teachers who may not set foot in the classroom at all but who may spend considerable periods of time in discussion with colleagues on ways in which the curriculum can be made more accessible to all children in the class, including the least able. Such discussions may involve an examination of textbooks and other reading assignments for readability, conceptual difficulty and relevance of content, as well as issues concerned with the presentation of the material, language modes and complexity used to explain what is required, and the use of different approaches to teacher–pupil dialogue.

IMPLICATIONS FOR TEACHER TRAINING

Issues of training are raised by the authors of the three overview works in this series but permeate all the volumes concerned with specific areas of the curriculum or specific areas of special needs.

The scale and complexity of changes taking place in the field of special needs and the necessary transformation of the teacher-training curriculum imply an agenda for teacher training that is nothing less than retraining and supporting every teacher in the country in working with pupils with special needs.

Although teacher training represented one of the three major priorities identified by the Warnock Committee, the resources devoted to this priority have been meagre, despite a strong commitment to training from teachers, LEAs, staff of higher education, HMI and the DES itself. Nevertheless, some positive developments can be noted (for more detailed accounts of developments in teacher education see Sayer and Jones, 1985 and Robson, Sebba, Mittler and Davies, 1988).

Initial training

At the initial training level, we now find an insistence that all teachers in training must be exposed to a compulsory component concerned with meeting special needs in the ordinary school. The Council for the Accreditation of Teacher Education (CATE) and HMI seem set to enforce these criteria; institutions that do not meet them will not be accredited for teacher training.

Although this policy is welcome from a special needs perspective, many questions remain. Where will the staff to teach these courses come from? What happened to the Warnock recommendations for each teacher-training institution to have a small team of staff specifically concerned with this area? Even when a team exists, they can succeed in 'permeating' a special needs element into initial teacher training only to the extent that they influence all their fellow specialist tutors to widen their teaching perspectives to include children with special needs.

Special needs departments in higher education face similar problems to those confronting special needs teams in secondary schools. They need to gain access to and influence the work of the whole institution. They also need to avoid the situation where the very existence of an active special needs department results in colleagues regarding special needs as someone else's responsibility, not theirs.

Despite these problems, the outlook in the long term is favourable. More and more teachers in training are at least receiving an introduction to special needs; are being encouraged to seek out information on special needs policy and practice in the schools in which they are doing their teaching practice, and are being introduced to a variety of approaches to meeting their needs. Teaching materials are being prepared specifically for initial teacher-training students. Teacher trainers have also been greatly encouraged by the obvious interest and commitment of students to children with special needs; optional and elective courses on this subject have always been over-subscribed.

Inservice courses for designated teachers

Since 1983, the government has funded a series of one-term full-time courses in polytechnics and universities to provide intensive training for designated teachers with specific responsibility for pupils with special needs in ordinary schools (see *Meeting Special Needs in Ordinary Schools* by Seamus Hegarty in this series for information on research on evaluation of their effectiveness). These courses are innovative in a number of respects. They bring LEA and higher-education staff together in a productive working partnership. The seconded teacher, headteacher, LEA adviser and higher-education tutor enter into a commitment to train and support the teachers in becoming change agents in their own schools. Students spend two days a week in their own schools initiating and implementing change. All teachers with designated responsibilities for pupils with special needs have the right to be considered for these one-term courses, which are now a national priority area for which central funding is available. However, not all teachers can gain access to these courses as the institutions are geographically very unevenly distributed.

Other inservice courses

The future of inservice education for teachers (INSET) in education in general and special needs in particular is in a state of transition. Since April 1987, the government has abolished the central pooling arrangements which previously funded courses and has replaced these by a system in which LEAs are required to identify their training requirements and to submit these to the DES for funding. LEAs are being asked to negotiate training needs with each school as part of a policy of staff development and appraisal. Special needs is one of nineteen national priority areas that will receive 70 per cent funding from the DES, as is training for further education (FE) staff with special needs responsibilities.

These new arrangements, known as Grant Related Inservice Training (GRIST), will change the face of inservice training for all teachers but time is needed to assess their impact on training opportunities and teacher effectiveness (see Mittler, 1986, for an interim account of the implications of the proposed changes). In the meantime, there is serious concern about the future of secondments for courses longer than one term. Additional staffing will also be needed in higher education to respond to the wider range of demand.

An increasing number of 'teaching packages' have become available for teachers working with pupils with special needs. Some (though not all) of these are well designed and evaluated. Most of them are school-based and can be used by small groups of teachers working under the supervision of a trained tutor.

The best known of these is the Special Needs Action Programme (SNAP) originally developed for Coventry primary schools (Muncey and Ainscow, 1982) but now being adapted for secondary schools. This is based on a form of pyramid training in which co-ordinators from each school are trained to train colleagues in their own school or sometimes in a consortium of local schools. Evaluation by a National Foundation for Educational Research (NFER) research team suggests that SNAP is potentially an effective approach to school-based inservice training, providing that strong management support is guaranteed by the headteacher and by senior LEA staff (see Hegarty, *Meeting Special Needs in Ordinary Schools*, this series, for a brief summary).

Does training work?

Many readers of this series of books are likely to have recent experience of training courses. How many of them led to changes in classroom practice? How often have teachers been frustrated by their inability to introduce and implement change in their schools on returning from a course? How many heads actively support their staff in becoming change agents? How many teachers returning from advanced one-year courses have experienced 'the re-entry phenomenon'? At worst, this is quite simply being ignored: neither the LEA adviser, nor the head nor any one else asks about special interests and skills developed on the course and how these could be most effectively put to good use in the school. Instead, the returning member of staff is put through various re-initiation rituals ('Enjoyed your holiday?'), or is given responsibilities bearing no relation to interests developed on the course. Not infrequently, colleagues with less experience and fewer qualifications are promoted over their heads during their absence.

At a time of major initiatives in training, it may seem churlish to raise questions about the effectiveness of staff training. It is necessary to do so because training resources are limited and because the morale and motivation of the teaching force depend on satisfaction with what is offered — indeed, on opportunities to negotiate what is available with course providers. Blind faith in training for training's sake soon leads to disillusionment and frustration.

For the last three years, a team of researchers at Manchester University and Huddersfield Polytechnic have been involved in a DES funded project which aimed to assess the impact of a range of inservice courses on teachers working with pupils with special educational needs (see Robson, Sebba, Mittler and Davies, 1988, for a full account and Sebba, 1987, for a briefer interim report). A variety of courses was evaluated; some were held for one evening a week for a term; others were one-week full time; some were award-bearing, others were not. The former included the North-West regional diploma in special needs, the first example of a course developed in total partnership between a university and a polytechnic which allowed students to take modules from either institution and also gave credit recognition to specific Open University and LEA courses. The research also evaluated the effectiveness of an already published and disseminated course on behavioural methods of teaching — the EDY course (Farrell, 1985).

Whether or not the readers of these books are or will be experiencing a training course, or whether their training consists only of the reading of one or more of the books in this series, it may be useful to conclude by highlighting a number of challenges facing teachers and teacher trainers in the coming decades.

1. We are all out of date in relation to the challenges that we face in our work.

2. Training in isolation achieves very little. Training must be seen as part of a wider programme of change and development of the institution as a whole.
3. Each LEA, each school and each agency needs to develop a strategic approach to staff development, involving detailed identification of training and development needs with the staff as a whole and with each individual member of staff.
4. There must be a commitment by management to enable the staff member to try to implement ideas and methods learned on the course.
5. This implies a corresponding commitment by the training institutions to prepare the student to become an agent of change.
6. There is more to training than attending courses. Much can be learned simply by visiting other schools, seeing teachers and other professionals at work in different settings and exchanging ideas and experiences. Many valuable training experiences can be arranged within a single school or agency, or by a group of teachers from different schools meeting regularly to carry out an agreed task.
7. There is now no shortage of books, periodicals, videos and audio-visual aids concerned with the field of special needs. Every school should therefore have a small staff library which can be used as a resource by staff and parents. We hope that the present series of unit texts will make a useful contribution to such a library.

The publishers and I would like to thank the many people – too numerous to mention — who have helped to create this series. In particular we would like to thank the Associate Editors, James Hogg, Peter Pumfrey, Tessa Roberts and Colin Robson, for their active advice and guidance; the Honorary Advisory Board, Neville Bennett, Marion Blythman, George Cooke, John Fish, Ken Jones, Sylvia Phillips, Klaus Wedell and Phillip Williams, for their comments and suggestions; and the teachers, teacher trainers and special needs advisers who took part in our information surveys.

Professor Peter Mittler   University of Manchester
                                                          January 1987

REFERENCES

Clunies-Ross, L. and Wimhurst, S. (1983) *The Right Balance: Provision for Slow Learners in Secondary Schools*. Windsor: NFER/Nelson.
Committee of Inquiry (1985) *Education for All*. London: HMSO (The Swann Report).

Croll, P. and Moses, D. (1985) *One in Five: The Assessment and Incidence of Special Educational Needs*. London: Routledge and Kegan Paul.

Farrell, P. (ed.) (1985) *EDY: Its Impact on Staff Training in Mental Handicap*. Manchester: Manchester University Press.

Hanko, G. (1985) *Special Needs in Ordinary Classrooms: An Approach to Teacher Support and Pupil Care in Primary and Secondary Schools*. Oxford: Blackwell.

Hargreaves, D. (1982) *Challenge for the Comprehensive School*. London: Routledge and Kegan Paul.

Hodgson, A., Clunies-Ross, L. and Hegarty, S. (1984) *Learning Together*. Windsor: NFER/Nelson.

Inner London Education Authority (1984) *Improving Secondary Education*. London: ILEA (The Hargreaves Report).

Inner London Education Authority (1985a) *Improving Primary Schools*. London: ILEA (The Thomas Report).

Inner London Education Authority (1985b) *Equal Opportunities for All?* London: ILEA (The Fish Report).

Mittler, P. (1986) The new look in inservice training, *British Journal of Special Education*, **13**, pp. 50–51.

Muncey, J. and Ainscow, M. (1982) Launching SNAP in Coventry. *Special Education: Forward Trends*, **10**, pp. 3–5.

Robson, C., Sebba, J., Mittler, P. and Davies, G. (1988) *Inservice Training and Special Needs: Running Short School-Focused Courses*. Manchester: Manchester University Press.

Sayer, J. and Jones, N. (eds) (1985) *Teacher Training and Special Educational Needs*. Beckenham: Croom Helm.

Sebba, J. (1987) The development of short, school-focused INSET courses in special educational needs. *Research Papers in Education* (in press).

Topping, K. and Wolfendale, S. (eds) (1985) *Parental Involvement in Children's Reading*. Beckenham: Croom Helm.

Wedge, P. and Prosser, H. (1973) *Born to Fail?* London: National Children's Bureau.

Widlake, P. (1984) *How to Reach the Hard to Teach*. Milton Keynes: Open University Press.

Widlake, P. (1985) *Reducing Educational Disadvantage*. London: Routledge and Kegan Paul.

Preface

The relatively narrow intellectual developments, which have for so long been the dominant stock in trade of the teaching profession, far too frequently subordinate, or drive out, consideration of students' social and emotional development. The cry that we need more and more scientists and technicians contributes to this undervaluing of the arts. A school with ten thousand pounds worth of computing equipment and insufficient poetry, paint, paste, puppets, plays or paper, is a sad place.

The vehicles of the creative arts are valid means of both intellectual and emotional development. Sadly, in many comprehensive schools they are more frequently neglected than capitalised upon. The 'back to basics' cry that is heard whenever the sacred cow of attainments is thought to be ailing is often one of despair, in so far as students with special needs in ordinary secondary schools are concerned. Students in many secondary school classrooms are literally told to 'shut up' and are metaphorically immured in emotionally and intellectually impoverishing environments. The absenteeism records in our secondary schools bear eloquent testimony to this assertion.

Teachers have been aware of the importance of the emotions in any educative process. Recent examples include Sybil Marshall and David Holbrook and, now, Bernadette Walsh. Bernadette Walsh has demonstrated in a comprehensive school that students with special needs possess abilities and sensitivities that can be capitalised upon to a degree that many members of the teaching profession would find incredible.

The material she presents, drawn from her work with such students, demonstrates what needs to be done and what can be achieved. The task required knowledge of both one's subject and one's students. These are necessary but not sufficient conditions for the processes and successes that Bernadette Walsh and her students so vividly demonstrate. The essential characteristics of the effective communicator are also required: the ability to listen, to empathise and to encourage. And underpinning these attributes is a fervent belief in the potentialities of all her students and the value of education. These are important lessons for all teachers interested in improving the quality of secondary education.

Peter D. Pumfrey   University of Manchester

Introduction

We cannot communicate. We never could.

(The Pinballs, Betsy Byars)

To add yet another book on 'communication' to this already over-subscribed aspect of the curriculum may seem at first superfluous. But there is a deepening ambiguity in the concept of 'communication' when applying it to pupils with special needs in the secondary school. Gusdorf (1953) defined this concept thus:

> True communication is the realization of a unity i.e. a piece of common labour. It is the unity of each with the other, but at the same time the unifying of each with himself, the re-arrangement of personal life in the encounter with others. I cannot communicate as long as I do not try to bring to the other the profound sense of my being.
>
> (Gusdorf, 1953, p. 57)

Here Gusdorf was presenting a definition of communication as an encounter between persons. It is language which marks out the point of encounter between self and others. Similarly, and more recently, Wilkinson presented a proposition: I communicate therefore I am. In this, he suggested that one exists not as a physical being, but 'as a personality, and a social being, with a self-image and identity in the social world' (Wilkinson, 1985, p. 66).

These considerations imply that each of us realises the self through language, and at the same time, language growth is that which marks out the point of encounter between the self and others in an open relationship. It is primarily through communication of one form or another that the web of human relationships is created and maintained. Some pupils with special needs, however, are often the victims of a lack of communication throughout their learning experience. This can be viewed not only in terms of the pupils' own language learning difficulties, but within the wider framework of the school curriculum and the learning relationships they encounter.

The Hargreaves Report to ILEA (1984) and the DES sponsorship of several local initiatives for low attainers, form part of the increasing attention now being paid to the needs of that large part of pupils in our schools for whom traditional curricula appear unsatisfactory. Reason for their lack of success are viewed not simply in terms of the pupils' ability, but as more closely related to the quality of the curriculum they are required to follow. A 'whole school approach' means that children with special needs should not be denied a fuller access to the mainstream curriculum. In English Studies, this is not always the case. The paucity of the English curriculum for such pupils has been substantiated by the research of Barnes and Barnes who found that:

> In general, however, there was evidence of lowered intellectual demands being made of bottom sets, and a prevalence of 'personal growth' and 'basic skills' approaches. Indeed it seemed that at fifth year level only bottom sets spent time practising written conventions. As we saw in some school syllabuses, there was a tendency to conceive more narrowly the needs of less able pupils with an emphasis on conventions and low-level instrumental competencies such as form-filling.
>
> (Barnes and Barnes, 1984, p. 381)

Such a curriculum offers little to the pupils' subjective, emotional development. As a result, pupils with special needs often form a hybrid group of individuals whose problems are not regarded as having emotional roots. Their difficulties range from timidity and being withdrawn to a general disaffection with school. Pupils invariably reveal such disaffection either through bored apathy or by a display of aggressive, anti-social behaviour.

In contrast to this impoverished curriculum of course texts and exercises, there is now an increasing awareness that English should be seen as an art, that is, a creative discipline (Abbs, 1982; Harrison, 1983a). An arts-based English curriculum offers creative extensions and a creative discipline to a child's language through the creating and telling of stories, poems, plays and so on — in short, through art-discourse. Because our language has a poetic basis, it seeks embodiment in many forms of expression — spoken, musical, written and painted.

This book emphasises the importance of the arts and their influence upon the affective development of secondary school pupils with special educational needs.

Chapter 1 sets out to show the necessity of small group talk within the English curriculum. It illustrates how talk is the primary means through which learning relationships are established and maintained.

In Chapter 2, communication through the narrative arts is explored. Emphasis is put upon the importance of introducing literature of quality to children with special educational needs. The possibility and appropriateness of approaching texts through the medium of film is explored. The value of 'paired reading' is also demonstrated.

For many children with special educational needs, writing can become an elusive skill. In Chapter 3, it is shown how writing can be used to encourage pupils to write from their personal centres of experience in a therapeutic way.

The expressive disciplines of drama, dance, music, puppetry, photography and visual art are shown in Chapter 4 to be the means by which the English curriculum for pupils with special educational needs can be broadened.

The concluding chapter argues the place of arts experience as central to the curriculum for pupils with special educational needs.

UNDERSTANDING THE UNSAID

Pupils with special needs frequently have a poor self-image, not unlike that portrayed by D. H. Lawrence's fictitious character, Tom. This is how Lawrence (1915) described him:

> He could not learn deliberately. His mind simply did not work. In feeling he was developed, sensitive to the atmosphere around him, brutal perhaps, but at the same time delicate, very delicate. So he had a low opinion of himself. He never knew his own limitation. He knew that his brain was a slow hopeless good-for-nothing. So he was humble.
>
> But at the same time his feelings were more discriminating than those of most of the boys, and he was confused. He was more sensuously developed, more refined in instinct than they. For their mechanical stupidity he hated them, and suffered cruel contempt for them. But when it came to mental things, then he was at a disadvantage. He was at their mercy.
>
> (Lawrence, 1915, p. 16)

Lawrence's sensitive and sympathetic insight towards his character, Tom, serves to highlight some contemporary attitudes to such pupils in schools. Teachers communicate directly to their pupils through what they teach or by what they deliberately require their pupils to learn. There is also the indirect, but still purposely planned provision of a particular type of learning environment or atmosphere organised to encourage learning. More important, is the learning that 'rubs off' on pupils as a result of teachers being the individuals that they are and the attitudes that they convey to their pupils. Dunlop (1984) has put renewed emphasis on the aspect of the learning environment which has in the past been referred to as 'the hidden curriculum'; the area where learning is 'sparked off' and transmitted in an indirect way. He argued that the 'hiddenness' of curricula is an essential component of the arbitrary conditions that make people what they are. The notion of a 'hidden curriculum' although not particularly 'fashionable' these days, is not new—earlier contributions by Hargreaves (1976) testify to this. The 'hidden curriculum' is a complex and important element of the phenomena of schooling. An awareness of it helps in understanding the attitudes communicated within it to children with special needs. The plight of the low achiever has been the focus of a later contribution from Hargreaves (1980). In *'Social Class, the curriculum and the lower achiever'*, he first invoked Holt's view (1965) that a main effect of the 'hidden curriculum' is to inspire fear — of one's self, or failure — of whatever has to be learned. He then went on to argue that such pupils would be helped if there was more attention on the 'aesthetic–artistic, the affective–emotional, the physical–manual and the social inter-personal' which are now always assigned an inferior position to the 'intellectual–cognitive' aspects of the curriculum. Within the 'hiddenness' of the curriculum, pupils with special needs implicitly pick up messages that they are failures. Through what remains unsaid, these children often develop, and have confirmed by the reflection they perceive, a low opinion of their own worth. They are indeed 'shut up' through being suppressed whether at a personal or curriculum level, or by institutionalised regimes.

There can be no doubt that one of the most significant consequences of the 1981 Education Act lies in the fact that pupils' special needs should, in future, be seen in a positive educational context rather than on a disability model which contributes little to improving learning. Though the emphasis would appear to be placed upon the individual's need rather than upon the handicap, with pupils who have language learning difficulties, the curriculum offered to them is often limited in its horizon. It is often unrelated either to the basic need of an individual — a trusting pupil–teacher relationship for example — or to the longer-term need of the pupil. To give a practical application by way of an example: for the pupil with learning difficulties in reading, the goal is often for him or her to achieve a prescribed reading age on current tests even though this attainment is not sufficient to meet many of the demands of secondary school texts. Once this prescribed level is reached, all too often, support is withdrawn too soon and too abruptly and we are then surprised that the pupil with learning difficulties does not continue to make progress. Even if this prescribed level of proficiency in reading has been reached, pupils after the third year in the secondary school may cease to receive support simply because there is no provision beyond a certain age.

Invariably, pupils with special needs spend too much of their time working on aspects on which they are failing. In part, this is why truancy and disaffection with school increase. Too little attention is paid to ways of introducing pupils to literature for example, of which their reading difficulties may have deprived them. Access to talk, drama, television, film, video and dance in order to widen the pupils' otherwise limited educational experience may be an important aspect for which the teacher of pupils with special needs could make provision. With few exceptions, English work for these pupils has focused on 'the basics' with concentration on out-of-context literacy skills, particularly in reading, writing and spelling. While not denying the necessity of such skills, our concern should be a practical matter of how these skills are best achieved. Such 'hair-of-the-dog' principles are likely to be of limited success beyond a certain age, when all they do for pupils is to reinforce a sense of failure. Where this approach may be effective is with those who have genuinely missed a crucial stage of schooling, but will be of limited success with those pupils who have 'given up' through repeated failure.

Central to the special needs curriculum in many schools, is still a notion of discrepancy — the discrepancy, for instance, between apparent mental ability and attainment. The implication is that the difficulties which many pupils have with basic skills stems from some kind of individual failure in their learning processes. Underlying this central concept is an ideology which suggested that there is a level of functioning which may be regarded as 'normal' or at least 'desirable'. Quasi-medical terms such as 'diagnosis', 'treatment' and 'screening' are used to describe the pupils' difficulties as if they are a pathological condition. This 'ideology of pathology' was a point raised by Gordon and Wilcox who suggested that such strategies and attitudes have also contributed to the low esteem and poor performance of many pupils. They go on to say:

> A deficit model of children — 'there's something wrong with them' — based on a quasi-medical approach to identification and treatment of symptom-problems has been the core of this practice. We have constructed elaborate systems for categorizing children, devised lengthy and most impressive diagnostic instruments and have produced expensive kits and materials to treat these identified symptoms.
> It is hardly surprising therefore, that remedial teachers are dismayed and perplexed by the discouraging conclusions of research projects, national surveys and their own colleagues, concerning their efficacy. The underlying causes of difficulty are still present despite the expensive prescription-pad treatment — 'a digraph a day keeps dyslexia away?'
>
> (Gorden and Wilcox, 1983, p. 47)

Clearly, this is not the same principle of healing as suggested by Hourd (1951) in *Learning Health and Learning Illness*. She argued that learning-health is established when both the teacher and pupil work from the capacity for all knowledge. Such is the very essence of the 'whole school approach' whereby pupils with special needs are given access to a broad curriculum with a rich choice of learning opportunities. Effecting changes to accommodate a 'whole-school approach' is not going to happen quickly. Pupils with special needs are still being withdrawn mercilessly from mainstream classes. The purpose of withdrawal is supposedly to enable attention to be directed towards the pupils' weaknesses in basic skills. The object of the attention is to return the pupils as soon as possible to what is regarded as 'normal' functioning. The role of the special needs teacher in this sense, is one of expert in the application of a diagnostic approach to reading and writing, rather than that of enabler or facilitator towards the broader aspects of the learning environment. Gordon had comments to make on the practice of withdrawal. He suggested that the very act of withdrawal from the ordinary class (Gordon and Wilcox, 1983), even for a short assessment, is often a shaming experience for young people. This is counter to the spirit of the 1981 Education Act. Circular 1/83, for example, which considered the implications of the Act, stated:

> The feelings and perceptions of the child concerned should be taken into account, and the concept of partnership should, wherever possible, be extended to older children and young persons.
>
> (DES, 1983, p. 2, para. 6)

The practical illustrations used throughout this book draw from a variety of grouping models for teaching pupils with special educational needs. Much is support teaching in mainstream, mixed-ability classes where some pupils were following a GCSE course while others were not taking a public examination (see Chapters 1, 2 and 3). Other examples come from withdrawal groups of 'lower band' pupils (Chapter 4). Single pupils with more severe learning difficulties or those with problems of emotional adjustment were both counselled and taught on a one-to-one basis (see Chapters 2 and 3).

WHO HAS SPECIAL EDUCATIONAL NEEDS?

To answer this question, one must admit that all pupils have certain needs. If pupils are to fulfil their potential, then these needs must be met for all pupils. When we aspire to meeting the needs of all pupils, it inevitably follows that we must be meeting the sub-set of needs regarded as 'special'. Full participation in many secondary school subjects, for example, requires a certain level of literacy, a level often determined by the subject itself and the media through which it is taught. In many subject areas, teachers who are not specifically involved with special needs have come to assume that pupils with learning difficulties are not their concern. Some do not regard it as their role to adapt material to the abilities of these pupils. In such cases, to be accepted, involves the pupils being able to meet the literacy demands within these specific subjects areas as they stand at present. Many pupils with special needs require adapted curricula as the reading demands posed by both printed texts and teacher-produced worksheets may effectively exclude pupils from full participation in the curriculum.

Where there is a heavy focus on literacy being regarded as a service skill to the rest of the mainstream curriculum, an impossible burden is placed on the special needs teachers. This is because the teachers are required to produce literary competence in their pupils out of context with the subject areas themselves. A disproportionate amount of time is then given to teaching the skills of reading and writing in the form of 'compensatory language programmes' with emphasis firmly placed on the mechanics of such skills. The skills of using language through talk are essential prerequisites for reading with understanding: yet talk as a means of encouraging pupils with special needs to communicate is still not included as much as it could be.

TEACHER-ENABLER

Teachers responsible for special needs may take classes labelled with many euphemisms. Such variety serves to reflect also the diversity of organisation, staffing and function both at local level and within each individual school. Such provision may be given in full or part-time units, or to groups of pupils extracted regularly from timetabled classes. A more enlightened approach is to have extra support within mainstream classes within a 'whole-school policy'. Often, the one unifying factor in the multiplicity of names and organisations is the attempt on the part of the teacher to 'remedy' the pupils' lack of measurable educational progress. In this sense, the 'remedial' or 'special needs' department is justifiably regarded as an 'ambulance service' to the rest of the curriculum.

In addition, since the implementation of the 1981 Education Act, it is gradually being envisaged that more pupils whose needs were once met in special schools will, in the future, become integrated into ordinary schools. It is also stressed that special education is considered only as a temporary provision for some pupils. Return to the ordinary school is a goal for a greater proportion of those assessed at some time as in need of special education. For such developments to take place, there are implications for 'remedial' teachers with many taking on a modified or dual role as 'co-ordinator for children with special education needs', 'support teacher' or some similar title.

It is certainly true that many pupils who might otherwise be in special schools are retained in ordinary schools. There are also many pupils in ordinary schools with as severe learning difficulties as those in special schools. Sometimes, the decisive factor determining referral is not so much the pupil's learning difficulties but the accompanying behavioural difficulties or perhaps the lack of appropriate support in schools.

There is an inter-relatedness between 'remedial' and special education. This has forced teachers to take account of the implications created by the greater integration and re-integration of pupils who might previously have been in full-time special education. 'Remedial' education now has to reconsider its earlier generally accepted nature in order to meet newly found roles. Clark (1975) provided a forcible prophecy:

> Unless remedial specialists are alert to the implications for them of new developments such as these in education, they may awake to discover that integration of handicapped pupils in ordinary schools has gradually and therefore imperceptibly changed the type of children for whom they are responsible so that they have become a cheaper and less well supported form of 'special education' contained within the ordinary school.
>
> (Clark, 1975, p. 7)

The real role of the teacher with responsibility for special educational needs is to enable the pupils to have a fuller access to an enriched curriculum. Such teachers are seen also to enable colleagues to present their curricula in ways in which they are more accessible to all pupils. The way forward is to be teacher-enablers.

Since the 1981 Education Act, schools are having to make considerable modification to the types of courses now provided. The expertise of the special needs teacher may well be at a higher premium than at any other time. One of the ultimate aims of special needs is the eventual phasing-out of 'remediation'. Instead, it is, in some instances, seeking to broaden its scope by permeating and integrating with the mainstream of education.

DISMANTLING THE RAINBOW

Within English Studies, concern about the separation of pupils with special needs from ordinary class experience found clear expression in the Bullock Report (1975):

Children who are in need of special help sometimes have their weaknesses exposed by the very efforts designed to remedy them, particularly if these result in fewer opportunities to achieve success in other activities such as Art, Craft, Drama and Music. This can be particularly true of older children for whom a monotonous and prolonged emphasis on remedial work in the basic skills occupies a major portion of the time. Where this is at the expense of other parts of the curriculum, which may offer them a greater chance of success, the policy can be self-defeating.

(DES, 1975, p. 271–2)

Such comment, as the research by Barnes and Barnes (1984) evidenced, still has application, particularly to secondary pupils, who are beyond the age at which most pupils have mastered 'basic skills'. These children's 'failure' to acquire sufficient competence in literacy has proved a barrier to full participation in broader curriculum experiences.

It has been argued that special needs has concerned itself with the underachievement of pupils in basic skills, usually with children of 'low ability' as measured by objective tests. This narrow view provides a neat area for teachers in which to operate, and may therefore account for its wide acceptance in schools. By gauging the disparity of their pupils' scores with national norms in IQ and basic attainment tests, teachers had 'cut-and-dried' terms of reference — to raise standards to the level of 'normality'. Surely this is searching for the pot of knowledge at the end of the educational rainbow? In so striving, are not the more fundamental needs of the pupils being overlooked? For the one feature that most children with learning difficulties share is their utterly negative view of self. They lack, almost entirely, a sense of self-worth. From the vast upsurge in literature about the organisation of special educational needs which has appeared currently on the British scene, the collective attitude conveyed is that children with learning difficulties can be 'managed' rather than understood as individual human beings.

An illuminating Canadian contribution can be found in the work of Weber (1974; 1982). Though he puts undue emphasis on the cognitive growth of learners through creative problem-solving techniques, he acknowledged the special needs pupils' capacity for a feeling-response towards poetry. He had this to say:

adolescent slower learners can *feel*. They are as capable of sensitivity and emotion as any of their more successful colleagues. And very often their sensitivity is even greater, or at least more honest, for slower learners react to poetry with a kind of unsophisticated candor that differs from the reaction of their academic colleagues who all too often express only what they are *supposed* to feel.

Why then, if slower learners are capable of emotion and feeling, do they so frequently gain a reputation as poetry-haters?

(Weber, 1974, p. 150)

The answer to this question perhaps lies in the false assumption that adolescents with learning difficulties are incapable of subtle feeling and that their experience of poetry, if this is presented to them at all, is never allowed to go beyond a few rugged narratives. It has been suggested that writing poetry is a first stage in encouraging the adolescents' appreciation and sensitivity towards the world (Weber, 1974). The scope of Weber's approach could only at best demonstrate his somewhat mechanical methods of encouraging poetry writing. He dwelt upon the aping of poetic forms instead of permitting his pupils to experience their own personal, living responses to the world. If poetry is to form the basis of the special needs English curriculum, then it can only come from the pupils' individual first-hand experience.

The subsequent work of Weber (1982) is similarly enlightening. In a memorable paragraph, he described the essential value of teachers and their relationship with those children experiencing difficulties:

> The teacher is the only one, in the chain of those responsible for this student, who has access to more than the technological data. The teacher is the only one with access to that student's pace and rhythm, fears and preferences, defences and mannerisms — all of which have a profound effect on achievement, but none of which can be tapped by technology. To rely entirely on technology heightens the potential for misdiagnosis, incorrect placement and inappropriate programming. It is simply not possible to reduce the needs of an exceptional student to a series of precise and measurable but fragmented and sterile objectives. Technology can help this student, but only if it is controlled by a sensitive teacher who combines it with intuition, understanding and, above all, common sense. Teaching and learning are dynamic human endeavours and they will always be so.
>
> (Weber, 1982, p. 12)

By implication, Weber is here stressing the importance of a warm, teacher–pupil relationship. In the same work, he suggested that all students need an advocate, a symphathetic listener, a mediator. While suggesting that 'the teacher is the key' to a pupil's learning, Weber's meaning is also that the teachers of special needs are responsible for presenting their pupils with structured skills programmes and learning packages which develop cognitive-thinking strategies. Thus, he does not confront the central issue: the need for a trusting teacher–pupil relationship as a basis for all learning.

It could be argued that the crucial contribution of special needs education is a therapeutic role, counselling and interpersonal relationships being seen as the key facets of remedial work. Warmth of personality and ability to give unquestioning acceptance to the pupil then become of prime importance as attributes in teachers responsible for helping children with learning difficulties. One critic (Collins, 1972, p. 9) spoke on behalf of many when he asked: 'Should we pretend that improvement can be brought about by the amateur therapy and brief coaching that passes for remedial education?' Can there be anything amateurish about entering into a relationship between the teacher and a pupil whose only handicap is a handicap of learning? Relationships based on mutual trust will inevitably be characterised by non-possessive, non-judgemental caring which can be found between therapist and patient, teacher and pupil (Rogers, 1983). This is a type of professional caring and concern that creates a safe atmosphere for the person seeking help. A genuine relationship will involve empathy and an accepting understanding of the inner world of the pupil. In this sense, the teacher becomes creative in facilitating learning in the pupil. The learning has a quality of involvement — the whole person being *in* the learning event. In this way, the pupil knows whether the learning experience is meeting her or his need and whether it is leading towards what each individual wants to know; whether it will illuminate the dark area of ignorance that the learner is experiencing. The learning then resides in the learner; its essence is meaning. When such learning takes place, the element of meaning to the learner is woven into the whole experience, so that the learning is a direct personal encounter.

SUMMARY

This chapter set out to define 'communication' as an encounter between people. It has been suggested that a consideration of language growth should take into account the complexity of relationships which develop. Pupils with special needs are often the victims of a lack of communication throughout their learning experience. This can be viewed not only in the light of the pupils' own language, but within the wider framework of the school curriculum and the learning relationships they encounter.

The curriculum on offer for children with special needs is often found to be limited in its horizon. Such a curriculum often focuses on 'the basics' of language at the expense of a more enriched curriculum such as an 'arts-based' approach to English Studies could offer.

Communication through Small Group Talk

> Well they say he can talk. He usually does talk, quite normally. But since he arrived at our house yesterday afternoon he hasn't said a word to anyone. He does as he's told, he eats his food and he dresses himself. But he doesn't say a word.
>
> (*The Trouble with Donovan Croft*, Bernard Ashley)

Significant changes in attitudes to children's talk occurred in the seventies, largely as a result of the pioneering work of Barnes (1976). Talk has moved from something to be forbidden towards a realisation that exploratory group talk was 'a good thing' to be encouraged at all costs. In the eighties, there was a re-emergence of concern about the scope and use of classroom talk in the light of the spoken component of the GCSE in English. Barnes' views are still naturally attractive as he raised a number of issues concerning classroom interaction. He showed the importance of relatively unstructured conversations in the nature of learning and emphasised that the inhibiting effect of rigid and formalised methods of teaching, which are in opposition to the natural pattern of enquiry, is the reason why many pupils seem to fail. He advocated small, interacting groups of pupils which utilise to the full a child's ability to take responsibility for his or her own learning. Barnes also stressed that the social organisation of the classroom must be planned and that the size of the group makes a difference to the opportunity for talk to develop. Four was considered to be the ideal number for small group talk. Barnes' evidence implied that the most favoured strategy for encouraging pupil talk is small group discussion where the pupils can learn from and with each other in discussing and talking around shared experiences. Such intimacy inhibits self-consciousness and encourages co-operative effort. Later work, and perhaps the most comprehensive study on this aspect is Barnes and Todd (1977) which acts as a fruitful culmination of some ten years' work in this area. It was found that groups of pupils working alone are likely to find exploratory talk available to them, if they know each other well. Because of the equal status and mutual trust the situation generates, it allows the children to be uncertain. This sort of activity encourages a tolerance of others as the group participants are seen as collaborators in a joint enterprise rather than as competitors for teacher approval. Present thinking remains sensitive to the need to promote talk in the classroom. In spite of this trend however, and though talk is often the most immediate form of communication for many pupils with special needs, it is still the most neglected part of their curriculum especially in the secondary school. Many of these pupils can contribute through talk with a confidence that is not apparent in their written work. Conversely, those pupils who do not willingly speak in group activities are likely to be at some disadvantage in their attempts to establish relationships. Certain individuals will have by their very nature, an innate predilection for keeping silent. This reserve — epitomised in the Yorkshire maxim 'ear all, see all and say nowt' — is characterised by a reluctance to speak except when absolutely necessary, and only then in terse replies. But in the classroom some pupils with special needs form their own 'culture of silence'. Keeping silent is often pupils' response to uncertainty in social relations. This unwillingness to speak and the reticence in social situations is exemplified by the withdrawn pupil who is reluctant to answer questions in class or to take part in classroom activities. For some pupils with special needs, their timidity, although similar to shyness, is probably somewhat more inclusive, as a degree of fear is revealed in certain learning encounters, especially when they experience something which is new or strange to them (Walsh, 1986). These pupils find the secondary school a bewildering place. Often a chat with a trusted teacher can be the first step to promoting the kind of talk so highly prized by the pupils during their English studies, as Jimmy's comments reveal:

Jimmy: I-I just know some o' teachers to say 'ello to and that's it. I don't stand and talk to 'em.
Teacher: Why do you think I give you a lot of opportunity for talking?
Jimmy: Like now, you sit and talk — 'cos — 'cos you let us talk in t'lesson.

Talk in school functions to create and establish relationships of one kind or another with an increasing circle of people. With every word that pupils utter, they reveal themselves to others, and in the human interplay, such utterances enable pupils to become social beings. The teacher is responsible for structuring the atmosphere of classroom relationships and, as was indicated in the introduction, every word, no matter how neutral or whatever the manner, exercises some effect upon personal relationships and upon learning. We show ourselves as individuals through talk. Not until we have done this can we establish our identity within a given group. Thus we place ourselves socially and psychologically in relation to each other through talk.

Our education is largely based on absorbing communications about experiences. With the growth of vocabulary, the clarity of understanding and the precision in usage, language will continue to improve. The moment that more than the minimum of words is used, some rules of grammar emerge and increase in range and complexity as the speaker's vocabulary expands further, while the observance of grammatical rules will become ever more precise. This is true in general for the discovery of learning skills. New principles make their appearances first in mere tendencies which are then sharpened and eventually consolidated (Chapter 3: *Communication through writing* will illustrate this more fully). It is the task of teachers to re-awaken these mere tendencies in their pupils as Warnock (1976) asserted:

> Children cannot be taught to feel deeply; but they can be taught to look and listen in such a way that the imaginative emotion follows.
>
> (Warnock, 1976, p. 7)

English is concerned with language as the expression of 'whole' experience, with bodily feelings and emotions; to live from the body's experience, is the true quest of language learning and teaching. The main concern of teachers of English is to develop in their pupils an acute sensitivity to poetic language, to what D. H. Lawrence called 'art speech'. This means encouraging a true aesthetic education which is committed to the expressive and inner life of the pupils. Such an approach should be no less available to children who experience learning difficulties. It is possible that, before they can gain access to more mature forms of language, it may be necessary for the teacher to help pupils to re-discover their world by re-awakening their sense of touch, vision, hearing, scent and taste. This awareness, first hand, is the essence of good Junior School practice, but it is a false assumption that all pupils in secondary school will have a rich store of such experiences on which to draw. This can be illustrated by the following extracts from the researcher's teaching journal. The group was mixed ability Fourth years:

18th September
After reading Dylan Thomas' Holiday Morning, I asked the group to write about their best holiday morning. Nicola had written about a day she spent in Castleton and had picked blackberries and bilberries. This event had evidently made a great impression on her and

subsequently, I felt that it should be developed in some way so that the class could share the pleasure of her experience. I began by reading Nicola's effort and then asked for other anecdotes concerning similar days in the countryside. Patrick mentioned that he had once picked blackberries, and so had Gerry, at a place near Lodge Moor, but in the entire group, no-one else had. I saw this as an opportunity to link the experience with Seamus Heaney's poem, 'Blackberry Picking'.

After reading the poem the group copied it out in 'best' handwriting. I noticed how very quiet the atmosphere had grown with all the pupils intent on this apparently mechanical activity. I then realised how valuable it could be to engage a class with this sort of work, but this was only as a preliminary to a development of a lesson — not an end in itself, as is often the case. When I asked the group to illustrate and decorate the margins of their paper, I soon understood that not many had a clear concept of what a blackberry looked like. This was my own fault, and I was justified in self-criticism here; it was obvious that very few of the pupils had first hand experience, yet I had expected them to undertake a task beyond their capability. The atmosphere was punctuated only by Gerry's occasional whistling. I intended to improve on my approach to this group during the next lesson.

19th September
This lesson was timetabled before lunch and as the day was so sunny, I told 4H that we weren't going to stay in for this lesson. 'Are we going to a football match?' 'No Gerry,' I said, 'we're going to look for some blackberries seeing that you're not sure what they look like.' 'Great!' he enthused.

We walked down the school path into the surrounding woods. Along a cinder path we saw some berries. I alerted the group's attention as to why Heaney had said that the berries were 'like eyes'. We collected some, putting them into a box. As we did, I noticed that the boys had been 'playing' at soldiers; Mark picking up a stick improvised and used it as a gun to shoot everyone in sight, and when I admonished Patrick's attempts at knocking down a tree for conkers, he reminded me that he was 'only playing'. Mark aimed a shot at a dog in a nearby garden thus bringing an angry reaction from a neighbour who then became 'the enemy'.

While Susan climbed to the top of the embankment in order to collect the best berries, Sharon confided that she hadn't picked blackberries before. 'Now you have', I assured her, 'look how stained your hands have become.' 'Yes, like red ink.' 'That would be a good description to write down when we get back to class, Sharon.'

We walked back through the garden from where Patrick helped himself to a stick of rhubarb. Suddenly something, whizzed past me, splattering at my feet. I looked down to find a squashed crab apple, a missile sent from the hand of Mark who explained that it was merely his 'hand-grenade'. 'Yes, you've blown the foot off my leg,' and I puzzled whether I was synonymous with 'the enemy' in Mark's mind.

Having returned to class where plain paper was given out, the blackberries were sketched and described. Sharon, Michelle and Nicola much to my delight, stayed behind after the lesson to ask for help in 'getting started'. I explored their own ideas through questions relating to the senses — colour, smell, taste — before sampling the berries. Marie had tried to wash them while they were still in the cardboard container. I felt I must re-read Macmurray's *Reason and Emotion* where he refers to sensitivity being developed through sensual awareness.

Realising that most of her class haven't experienced blackberrying as Sharon admitted, the teacher plans this experience for them first hand. The first times are an encounter through which new possibilities of extending feeling-in-language open up. Discovery through the senses and giving shape to these discoveries in language forms are bodily acts through which personal meanings are offered and shared.

Macmurray (1935) drew our attention to the need to educate our emotions, which means the cultivation of a direct sensitiveness to the reality of the world around us. This is achieved through our senses and sense experience. He suggested that the education of our emotional life is primarily an education of our sensibility:

> The fundamental element in the development of the emotional life is the training of this capacity to live in the senses, to become more and more delicately and completely aware of the world around us, because it is a good half of the meaning of life to be so. It is a training in sensitivity.
>
> (Macmurray, 1935, p. 44)

To help the pupils to develop an attitude of sensual receptivity, we can bring into the classroom things which are tangible: the pile of bones; heap of dead leaves; a flower; stones; shells; fir-cones; a candle; berries, all as fertile starting points for talking. In this next transcript, a selection of autumn berries was taken in to be explored before a more serious exploration of Heaney's poem began:

Samantha:	You can make sherry out of 'em.
Teacher:	You can make sherry out of the sloes can you?
Ann:	You can make jam.
Teacher:	Mm. And sloe gin as well can't you? That's right.
Ann:	Miss — what they called?
Teacher:	s-l-o-e sloe.
Ann:	s-l-o-e.
Teacher:	Alright and sloes is just an 's' on the end. Now I'd like you to think of some words and groups of words to

describe them and say them out aloud, if you like, and then see what you can say about them first of all and jot down any words that come to mind on your paper and then I'll come and join in the discussion in a minute or two.

(Teacher leaves group to discuss on their own.)

Immediately, the group show a quickened interest with what the teacher has presented them with. Samantha brings to the group her own personal knowledge: 'You can make sherry out of 'em' and this contrasts with Ann's response who has never come across sloes before and enquires: 'What are they called?' Realising this, the teacher uses the response to make explicit, incidentally almost, a new pattern of language to Ann, as the word is spelt out to her: 's-l-o-e' and 'sloes is just an 's' on the end.' She then invites the group as a whole to explore various patterns of language around the experience. There is no tedium connected with the chore of 'getting the spellings and words right'. It is all part of the language play within a living language. The teacher leaves the group to continue to talk and explore through language this experience. She provides the group with the opportunity to dare to explore in the full knowledge that she is there. The group begin talking on their own:

Jane:	Right — are you ready?
Ann:	No.
Richard:	No.
Jane:	Are we going round?
Ann:	What do you fink they are? Well this one's a sloe. You can make sherry out on' this one, and gin.
Jane:	Mm.

Through such exploration, confidence in new forms of language can quickly develop. Ann in particular showed an earlier uncertainty with this new experience but now she is handling it with confidence: 'this one's a sloe. You can make sherry out of this one, and gin.' She may in time, be able to cope with more complex associations: 'sloeblack, slow, black, crowblack, fishing-boat — bobbing sea.'

Ann:	And this one you can — it's elderberry — you can make jam — and wine.
Jane:	And jelly — you can make jelly. We were up in this orchard once, we helped this woman pick 'em 'cos she makes gallons and gallons of wine and I fink t' birds eat these — I don't know these things are ...

Samantha:	Red berries.
Ann:	Yeh — red berries. Ym-ym-ym-ym (laughs) wonder what they taste like — I'm not going to taste 'em I'll probably get poisoned. But you see this is all nature!
Jane:	Come on now.
Ann:	Samantha — what do you fink they are?
Samantha:	Things on trees.
Ann:	No but how — how would you describe 'em?
Samantha:	Little beads.
Jane:	We had a tray once.
Ann:	Yes and you should see all t' little birds in winter that try to come and find 'em pick 'em jub-b-b-bub.
Samantha:	Aah!

From their initial talk about sloes, the group then confidently explore the selection of other berries that have been made available for them: 'And this one you can — it's elderberry — you can make jam and wine.' The delight at this fresh awareness was not dissimilar to the rapture with which Marjory and Millicent in D. H. Lawrence's *Aaron's Rod* discover the coveted 'Blue Ball', the Christmas ornament which belonged to their father when he was a child. The sequence above has echoes of 'Now! What's this? — What's this? What will this beauty be?' (Chapter 1, p. 17). The group recall past experiences. Jane tells the group how 'we were up in an orchard once, we helped this woman pick 'em 'cos she makes gallons and gallons of wine'. Similarly, Ann remembers how birds come to the bird-tray during the winter.

There is an inherent energy in the talk. As the group grasp the moment of awareness, they pin it down in words, though sometimes the immediacy of the feeling can only be expressed in sounds 'jub-b-b-bub' and 'Ym-ym-ym-ym' or in body images in which gestures are used to indicate size, shape and texture:

Ann:	Er (laughs) it's horrible — it's messy in it? When you get 'em squashed — ugh! Bet it tasts nice though t'wine.
Jane:	You can make jam aht on 'em though and jelly.
Samantha:	You do — I can bring you some 'cos we make it.
Ann:	What — wine?
Samantha:	Got loads of it — we make a right — we make jam, sherry, wine, jellies all sorts with them and they grow to about that size (demonstrates size).
Ann:	Are they what people pinch out of your garden — yeh?
Samantha:	Yeh they're like grapes — you can, but not when they're right little, when they're that big (indicates size again).
Jane:	Are they nice when they're big?

Samantha:	Yeh — when we went to Italy we had 'em an' we went pickin' 'em.
Ann:	And didn't you bring 'em home?
Samantha:	We just ate 'em with custard — they stew 'em they stew 'em and put custard on.
Ann:	Do you put 'em in a pie?
Samantha:	No just eat 'em.
Ann:	God! ...

In such a non-threatening atmosphere, the group encourage one another to reveal that personal knowledge and experience which every child brings into the classroom. The talk is self-directing; they are responding actively and personally. In this activity, others are invited to participate. Samantha recalls her past experiences of picking berries in Italy. So absorbing is the game that later, Mark cannot resist enjoying the berries in a more realistic way by eating them, when Jane had merely desired them, saying 'I feel like eating 'em':

Ann:	God! Stephen what do you fink about.'em?
Stephen:	They're alright.
Ann:	What about you? Have you ever tasted any of 'em Jane?
Jane:	Na — ooh and I don't want to eever (either).
Ann:	I've tasted that elderberry but.
Samantha:	I'll try and bring some ...
Karen:	They look like grapes don't they?
Jane:	They do don't they?
Ann:	Grapes — they look like grapes.
Jane:	They look like grapes — I feel like eating 'em.
Samantha:	They'll be sour.
Ann:	But they're not nice — Miss Walsh said — look at that one — it's bad. Mark! (Mark eats a berry).
Jane:	Mark!
Ann:	And Mark Hunt has just eaten one of 'em.
Jane:	Shall I switch it off?
Stephen:	No.
Ann:	Yeh.

The talk captures the group engaging in language play. Almost without being conscious of the fact, they are creating their own living language: the berries 'look like grapes' and are 'little beads'. They draw upon their knowledge, 'You can make sherry out of 'em', and experiences of these natural forms, 'I've tasted that' and 'have you ever tasted 'em?' Because the reference to the berries is determined by the context, the group use deictics — pointing words — often referring to the objects by using a pronoun: 'They', 'this', 'that', 'these', 'them', 'those', 'it', 'em'; this makes the meaning of the talk impenetrable if heard out of context.

The writing from pupils with learning difficulties is invariably limited initially, but they gradually gain increasing confidence from an exploration of sensual imagery. First-hand experience through the senses enables them to attempt to write fresh, personal responses which are probably no more than the immediacy of sensual images as this piece from Michael indicates:

> Blackberries
> Little black and red balls
> They look like grapes
> And light is shining on them
> Birds eat them in Winter
> Because they have no more food
> Elderberries
> You can make wine from them
> Sloes
> Can be made into gin
> They are very spiky.
>   (Michael: fourth year)

This is no more than a compilation of some ideas suggested by the group, but Michael has ordered that sense awareness in a shape that becomes his own. Through first-hand experience and sharing through language, and through listening to and reading the writing from accepted writers, the pupils will gradually experience an increasing precision of thought, and a growing feeling not only for the lexical meaning of words, but for their value within a context. In addition, there seems to come a critical sense. They learn to weigh the effectiveness of an idea or an image: to reject the commonplace, the cliché, in favour of the effective image, the colour, texture, sound or taste that has the greatest possible impact. They will also enjoy themselves!

After this sort of exploration, the teacher introduces the group to a poem by Seamus Heaney entitled *Blackberrying*; it is given to them after they have experienced the writing process themselves:

Teacher: 81 ... page 81. You've been writing your own poems — I'd like you to have a look at this one now by someone called Seamus Heaney — there he is (points to photograph of poet in *Poetry Workshop* ed. M. and P. Benton).

Gregory: (in Irish accent) Seamus Heaney's Irish.

Teacher:	He is — now perhaps when I've read the poem, perhaps you could read a bit of it in an Irish accent (Teacher reads poem).
	Now what's that poem about?
Ian:	Blackberrying.
Teacher:	... what's it about?
Gregory:	Blackberrying.
Stephen:	They were going blackberrying but when they picked 'em they got thorns in their hands.
Teacher:	Yes.
Ann:	Miss — we had a right lot of blackberries but I sat on 'em and it were all over the chair.

Immediately, with Gregory's comment spoken in an Irish accent, that 'Seamus Heaney's Irish', it evidences a willingness to engage with the poem. The teacher invites him towards active involvement with the text by suggesting 'perhaps you could read a bit of it in an Irish acccent'. Further engagement with the text is shown through Stephen's reply 'They were going blackberrying but when they picked 'em they got thorns in their hands'. Here he is referring to the line in the poem 'Our hands were peppered with thorn pricks.' The poem re-awakened a similar experience when Ann comments 'We had a right lot of blackberries but I sat on 'em and it were all over the chair'. Relating the poem to their own experiences is a main way of the pupils coming to terms with the text. Benton (1986) refers to this as 'anecdotal paralleling' and throughout this exploratory talk there is considerable evidence to support his view that:

> It is essentially an anecdotal 'paralleling' of the central experience of the poem which helps them to 'place' it, to give it meaning within their own frames of reference and ultimately to show that, at one level at least, they 'possess' the poem even if a detailed analysis of it is beyond their powers ...
> ... This 'paralleling' activity might easily be dismissed by the casual listener as idle chat but close examination shows it to be reflecting central concerns of the poem and providing a means of relating it to the kind of knowledge and experience the children bring with them to the classroom.
>
> (Benton, 1986, p. 61–2)

This activity involves the pupils matching the patterns of experience re-counted in the poem with their own. The group in the above transcript relate Heaney's childhood memory to their own experiences of blackberry picking. From this early engagement, the teacher then guides the group towards a closer examination of the text:

Teacher:	And what happened to these blackberries?
Gregory:	They don't save.
Teacher:	They don't save, no, which line tells us not — which bit in particular?
Toni:	The last line of the first verse.
Teacher:	'Knew that they would not' yes what does that mean when it says 'we found a fur, a rat-grey fungus'.
Ann:	I thought they meant a rat at first.
Gregory:	Will you say it again Miss?
Teacher:	Yes — I ….
Richard:	They'd gone rotten.
Teacher:	There look when it says — they'd gone rotten hadn't they Richard — yes, 'We found a fur — a rat-grey fungus'.
Toni:	They'd gone bad.
Teacher:	They'd gone bad — yes because you know what happens to fruit when it goes bad?
Stephen:	Miss it guz all …
Mark:	Mouldy.
Teacher:	Mouldy, mm. Okay.

During such early stages of discussing a poem, the teacher's presence is felt, but not in a domineering manner implying that she knows all the answers. Her role is supportive as the group explores the poem. Occasionally, she repeats and reflects back their replies to convey the sense that the pupils' responses are accepted. In this way, the group feel secure enough to admit they have misinterpreted parts of the poem, for example when Ann declares: 'I thought they meant a rat at first' with reference to 'rat-grey fungus'. Also, Gregory asks 'Will you say it again Miss?' The teacher draws them even further towards a personal response:

Teacher:	… which lines in particular does anybody like? (Pause) So I've asked which lines or phrases anybody thinks are really good.
Stephen:	Miss.
Teacher:	Stephen.
Stephen:	That er — that third one.
Teacher:	Yes — which bit?
Stephen:	'At first …
Teacher:	… a glossy, purple clot — that's right and what does he say that it tasted like when he bit into that blackberry?
Stephen:	Wine.
Ann:	Like sweet …

Teacher: ... 'like sweet and thickened wine'.

This is a poem which easily reawakens past experiences. The group explore the poem through their sense awareness as they respond to the berries tasting 'like sweet and thickened wine'. The unfolding of the text has to be a gradual process with pupils with learning difficulties and the teacher's concern is to emphasise the value of the pupils' own personal experiences by next asking:

Teacher:	... Have many of you been blackberrying?
Voices:	Yeh.
Teacher:	Most of you have — where have you been?
Michael:	Miss.
Teacher:	Yes.
Michael:	In Wales we were picking 'em.
Ian:	(disbelieving tone) Oh!
Michael:	We were — Miss — squash 'em against car windahs.
Stephen:	Miss you know erm — have you ever heard of Adrian Minichello?
Teacher:	Yes.
Stephen:	Miss his dad guz blackberry picking and we used to go into t'wood and pick'em and we made wine ...
Teacher:	Lovely.
Stephen:	... and jam and that.
Teacher:	Good — so if you squash berries, Michael, on people's cars, does that explain why I got some squashed berries on my car the other day?
Michael:	I might had done it (causes laughter).
Teacher:	Might had done! I thought as much. I went through the car-wash and I thought: Well how on earth have these squashed berries got on top of the sun roof? So now the truth comes out doesn't it? (Teacher leaves group to discuss further before they attempt any more writing.)

It is tempting to ask what admitting to squashing berries on the teacher's car has to do with the poem, but it is precisely this sort of easy rapport and mutual acceptance that is essential to creating the safety-zone for pupils' feeling of confident response. There is space for joking and fun. Into this safety-zone comes their own experiences which are now publicly shared: 'his dad guz blackberry-picking and we used to go into t'woods and pick 'em and we made wine' and 'In Wales we were picking 'em'. With this discourse in particular, there is a homely feeling to it as individuals share their stories of how they 'made wine ... and jam and that'. The group continue to talk in the re-awakening encounter when the teacher leaves them:

Toni: The yew's a very nice shape. It's colourful and it's an evergreen.
John: Big like balls.
Richard: Shurrup! and it's like red-cherries and light green leaves.
Toni: And it looks like a summery type.
Ann: Yeh.
Toni: The leaves are shaped and fancy in a fancy way.
Ann: It looks colourful ... er.
Teacher: Alright — let's have you back in class.

In this sequence, the experience through sense awareness of the berries prompts the group to create descriptions of their own making, 'a summery type', for example demonstrates how individuals, pushed to the boundary of their language and understanding, will make up a word to express their feelings about objects being described. These are lexical innovations through which the children extend the meanings of words they know in order to express meanings for which they have no words. Clark (1983) says children 'are learning the process required in their language for creating new words'. Such inventiveness is not only how children extend their competence to make new meanings, it is also how any language renews itself — by means of metaphor. Gradually, the learner comes to know that there are accepted conventions for extending meaning, but the on-the-spot immediacy of the image, the 'firstness' of the perception which was expressed in the novelty of the words has gone. As the pupils learn more conventional forms of language, the 'firstness' of their feelings is edited out unless it is legitimised by writers of stories and poems and by teachers who understand the role of the imagination in the development of talk and learning.

When listening to the discourse, the teacher needs to be aware of instances when there is a grasping for a 'felt-thought', for at such times, the individual is trying to find a personal voice: this according to Heaney (1982) 'means that you can get your own feelings into your words and that your words have the feel of you about them'. Meek (1985) pointed to a link between children and poets in their use of language with respect to these 'first times', and the intuitive belief that poets and children seem to share, that words themselves have power and divination. The child experiences the 'first times' which the poet recreates as the shock of recognition. When the child's feelings are transposed into speech acts, this is language play. Equally, this same pleasure for creating language can be captured in early attempts at their own poems. In the next example, the group and their teacher had gone strawberry picking. Back in class they were invited to write their response.

> The strawberry big, red and plump
> small and rosary
> nice and tasty
> with the shape of a heart
> so red and plumpy
>
> strawberry strawberry
> strawberry nice and round
> nice and plumpy nice and red
> nice and big
> that lovely rosary red strawberry
> strawberry strawberry
> first they're there, then they're not.
>   (Toni: fourth year)

Words like 'rosary' and 'plumpy' show that Toni is trying to capture the shape, colour and texture of the fruit with language which is being stretched to the limits; then the shape is likened to a heart. As Toni strains to recapture the sensuous appeal of the strawberry she falls back upon incantatory repetitions which are reminiscent of early childhood words are repeated over and over again for the pleasure of hearing the sound.

VOICELESS POEMS

Not all pupils with special needs are eager to talk, even in small, intimate groups. Furthermore, until the teacher finds confidence to encourage small group talk, both require a more concrete focus for discussion than perhaps an exchange of anecdotal talk based on personal experience will allow. Writing about the use of pictures in the classroom, Creber (1979a; 1979b; 1985) reminded us that 'a picture is a voiceless poem; a poem is a vocal picture'. A picture, like film (see Chapter 2), can often become a text in itself. The children's response to a picture creates conditions in which the mind is free to reflect. This reflective mental play is possible if the teacher poses facilitating questions which will encourage the story-making activity. The following discussion took place after a group of fourth year girls

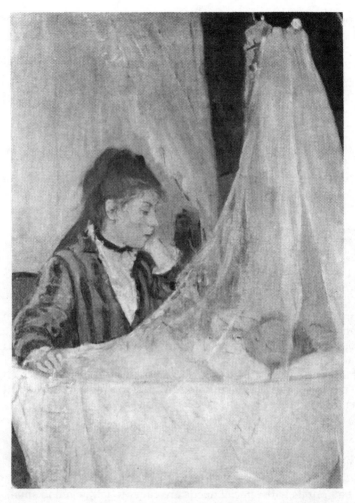

Berthe Morisot, Le Berceau. *Musée d'Orsay, Paris. Reproduced with permission.*

from a mixed ability group were discussing 'Le Berceau' by Berthe Morisot:

Teacher: So let's have a look at it. The first thing is, I want you to find out what is the relationship between that woman and the baby. How are they related do you think?

Patricia: It's her babby.

Teacher: You think that's her baby. How do you know that's not just a visitor?

Rachel: Aunty.

Teacher:	Mm. Maybe — and do you think it's a boy or a girl?
Patricia:	Girl.
Teacher:	Why's that?
Patricia:	Pink.
Teacher:	It's pink. Alright. Where do you think all this is taking place?
Katrina:	In a house, a big house.
Teacher:	In a bedroom or where?
Peggy:	Bedroom.

From quite specific, closed questions, which allow the group to deduce direct answers from the visual impact of the picture, the teacher gently persuades the discussion to more hypothetical replies through posing more open-ended questions:

Teacher:	And what are her feelings towards the baby? (Pause) What are her feelings ...
Katrina:	She loves it.
Teacher:	She loves it — how do you know?
Patricia:	You can tell how she's looking at it.
Teacher:	What do you think she is thinking about at the moment?
Patricia:	Ah! in't it luvverly? (giggles)

The teacher then invites the pupils through more facilitating questioning to engage in a story-making activity:

Teacher:	Do you think she might be preparing to leave?
Katrina:	Might be ...
Rachel:	Nah.
Teacher:	No?
Andrea:	She's come to see if it's alreight (alright)
Teacher:	And what do you think she might be hoping for the baby's future?
Rachel:	To be happy.
Andrea:	Happiness.
Patricia:	Beauty and reight (right) happy.
Teacher:	Beauty — good — anything else? Does she love the baby?
Katrina:	Yeh.
Teacher:	Katrina thinks she does.
Patricia:	Yeh.

Once this story-making activity has been encouraged, the girls quickly continue to fantasise about the woman's situation without needing as much direct prompting and guidance from the teacher:

Teacher:	Did she really want this baby?
Patricia:	No.
Andrea:	Nah.
Teacher:	Why not?
Patricia:	'Cos you can tell — she dun't look happy.
Katrina:	I think she wants it — she's just looking at it.
Rachel:	Nah I don't think she wants it.
Peggy:	No.
Rachel:	I think she's gooin' to gi' it away.
Andrea:	Aye.
Katrina:	I think she's going to put it up for adoption.
Teacher:	Mm.
Patricia:	I do.
Teacher:	Do you think ...
Patricia:	She might not be married.
Rachel:	Yeh and it was a disgrace in those days.
Andrea:	And she's wondering how she's going to do it.
Patricia:	I don't think she's married.

From an initial, coaxing comment from the teacher, the group gradually gain confidence which enables them to respond in ways which involve a wide range of mental activities through talk: speculating; connecting with own experiences; projecting; embroidering. The group's inventiveness was rooted in the experience of looking and talking allowing an exploratory response to develop before any writing is attempted. Through the consequent gain in confidence (including the use of tape-recorders) the group moved from a position where the context of the picture set limits to their possible response, to a position where the picture demanded reflective looking. There seems a clear connection here between that quality in reading which Lunzer and Gardner (1979) termed as a 'willingness to reflect'. The unusual ambiguity which visual material provides is what the teacher can utilise to good effect as starting points for group talk, especially as the response to pictures is an open-ended, individual matter. Because the responses are so personal, pupils with special needs do not feel threatened in any way, rather their individual contribution through talk is undisputably accepted.

SUMMARY

The importance of small group talk is discussed. It is suggested that in school, talk functions to create and establish relationships of one kind or another. It is seen to be the teacher's responsibility to structure the atmosphere of the classroom relationships, especially through talk. Learning is seen to be largely based on absorbing communications about experience. The need to encourage talk through first-hand experience should be given emphasis. Such an approach was then described in practical terms to involve the environment, poems, stories and pictures as starting points for small group talk. Thus can both emotional and intellectual needs be met. This is true of all pupils. Those deemed to have special needs are likely to have had a particularly restricted access to such experiences in formal education.

Communication Through the Narrative Arts

It has been one of the achievements of literature to make human beings aware of the fact that they are human. That's what it's all about. And I don't know anything else, particularly in the present age, makes you aware of that. Is sociology going to tell us that we are human? Is Psychology going to tell us — with the unique power that literature has — that we are human?

(*The Dean's December*, Saul Bellow)

Narrative arts — of talking, listening, reading, re-enacting, are essential to English Studies. In particular, the uses of fiction are acknowledged even in the joyless HMI Curriculum discussion document *English from 5 to 16* (DES, 1984) which recommends that older pupils should have 'some awareness of the relevance of imaginative literature to human experience', and that there should be experience of 'some literature and drama of high quality' so that ultimately, the habit of reading will be regarded as a source of pleasure and interest.

It has already been mentioned in the introduction that research from Barnes and Barnes (1984) suggests that such views are not wholly shared in practice by those who teach pupils with special needs. They found that literature is often considered only as the preserve of the 'examinable' pupils. The corollary of this being that 'non-examination' pupils, because of their apparent unsuitability to meet high examination standards are not introduced to literature of quality, and in some instances, not at all.

Fiction, drama or poetry if presented, are often made subservient to the interests of social issues, topicality and so forth; texts are justified on grounds of 'relevance' and 'social skills' rather than to any inherent narrative or imaginative merit. Consequently, a vast majority of secondary school pupils are presented with a sparse diet of books; they may never even glimpse stories that are genuinely 'relevant' to the complex, fascinating experience of being human, at both personal and social levels.

For those pupils with special needs placed initially in 'support' groups, the picture is even bleaker. Clunies-Ross and Wimhurst (1983) revealed how a large proportion of secondary schools select their pupils for extra help using non-verbal intelligence tests (still in use, if not in print, forty years on); and with an additional low score from a reading test to 'prove' it, there will be those identified as 'reluctant readers'. In meeting their special need, the goal is often for the pupil to reach a higher prescribed reading age — even though this in many cases, will still not meet the demands of many secondary school texts. In order to reach this coveted goal, it is likely that the pupils will have, until now, been set an educational task which will have involved them with phonics and flashcards, discrimination drills, diphthongs and diagraphs, matching cards, morphemes and structured reading programmes. The pupils will probably have been re-tested, and if they should by reading quotient show a slight improvement, it will be proof enough that it is due to the constant exposure the child has had to a systematic, structured programme of language drill. The programme is designed to get them through the test, but it is as though an 'L' driver was required to take a test without first having to drive 'in context' on the public road system.

By the time the pupil reaches fourth year, any impulse to learn which will once have existed may now be crushed. Why then, should approaches to reading as conditioned behaviour impress so much? Why, despite the evidence of failing practice with so called 'less able' readers, do we persist in the dull, daily routines of exercise-bound frustration? Who wouldn't be 'reluctant to read' if the sum total of an encounter with language followed the pattern just described? Kohl (1974) suggested that what should be easy and natural can be turned into a grim and tedious chore that makes no sense to the learner and therefore destroys motivation; but motivation he saw to be a false problem in this context:

> There is no need to motivate people to grow, and reading is part of growing in our culture. What might be necessary is negating the students' previous learning experience.
>
> (Kohl, 1974, p. 180)

To this end, *Skill Teach* (Shelton, 1984) provides an alternative reading resource for children with learning difficulties where other methods have proved unsuccessful. 'Paired Reading' (Morgan, 1976; Morgan and Lyon, 1979) holds possibilities, though the techniques used draw heavily upon behavioural theory, published accounts of which suggest the same obsession with testing. Pumfrey (1986) gave a lucid account of the possibilities and limitations of 'paired reading'. There are two distinct phases to this technique. In the first phase, the child chooses a book or other reading material. The adult care-giver (parent, teacher or older

'significant other') reads aloud all the words in the text simultaneously with the child. The child sets his or her pattern of pace and
rhythm to which the care-giver adjusts. In this way, the 'paired
reading' is synchronised. When the child makes an error, the
care-giver provides help and allows time for the child to repeat the
word correctly.

The second phase is that of independent reading by the child.
When the child feels ready to read aloud, he or she indicates this by
giving a previously agreed non-verbal signal such as a tap on the
table or a nudge. The signal must not interfere with the child's flow
of reading. The care-giver remains silent except for giving the
correct responses should the child make an error or is unable to read
a word. The correct response is repeated by the child and both child
and adult revert to simultaneous reading until the child signals for
the care-giver to stop.

This technique has been found to be effective with those pupils
who for whatever reason, have ceased to respond to other methods
of improvement. The success of this approach rests upon the
individual's personal choice of reading material and that of
establishing a trusting and supportive relationship between the
child and the helper, who in many cases, is the child's parent. From
the initial modelling by the child of a competent reader in phase one,
the child decides when he or she feels confident to 'go it alone'
through independent reading during phase two. Throughout, the
child's reading is positively reinforced by verbal praise, especially
when a word has been re-modelled by the care-giver. In addition,
'paired-reading' emphasises two principles: what we practise we
get good at and we enjoy doing what we are good at.

Pumfrey (1986) quite rightly called for caution and similarly
Swinson (1986) demonstrated that this approach is not without its
critics. It is suggested that 'paired-reading' shows no significant
difference in terms of improvement when compared with the more
traditional methods of involving parents just listening to their
children read. While no one would deny the success of conventional
strategies, one cannot escape the fact that with those children for
whom traditional methods fail, 'paired reading' has, according to its
more vocal proponents, proved to be a more effective method. It is
also true, that the young readers' confidence and enjoyment of
reading can be seen to increase from session to session.

It is noticed that with older pupils, quite a great deal of talk about
the chosen book is generated. Sometimes, it seems natural therefore
to intersperse the actual technique with a chat about the story. In
this way, there is opportunity for the pupils to match up the story
with their own experience, even though their attempts are tentative
at first. In the following transcript for example, Yvonne a fourth-

year pupil who had severe learning difficulties can identify with the main character of her chosen book *See You* by Joan Tate (Tate, 1984) because both have short hair:

Yvonne:	(reads) She brushed her short hair. She had always worn it ...
Teacher:	(adding intermittent praises) Well done — lovely.
Yvonne:	... very long, ever since her school days and only ...
Teacher:	(prompts) recently.
Yvonne:	(continues to read and indicates she wants to 'go it alone' again) only recently had had it cut shorter. A friend who was a hairdresser ...
Teacher:	Good.
Yvonne:	... had it done ...
Teacher:	Lovely.
Yvonne:	... and now it was like a cap that fitted her head. It was certainly easy to keep tidy.
Teacher:	Well done — that's tremendous! Did you always have short hair?
Yvonne:	No.
Teacher:	When did you have it cut?
Yvonne:	About seven.
Teacher:	When you were seven?
Yvonne:	About that yeh.
Teacher:	Mm. So you've always had it short while you've been at secondary school?
Yvonne:	Yeh.
Teacher:	Which do you prefer?
Yvonne:	Short.
Teacher:	Short. Good — alright — so.
Yvonne:	(continues with narrative) She brushed it straight and fair ...

Clearly Yvonne has not only found the confidence to read quite independently, but she is willing to discuss personal details about herself with the teacher as their mutual trust develops. The seeming 'luxury' of working with one pupil alone is something most teachers would see as logistically impossible. What needs to be pointed out is that like many other 'good ideas' this approach to reading depends very much on the goodwill of the care-giver devoting time away from the timetable. In this instance, Yvonne and the teacher met either during lunch-time, registration period or after school. If the claims for this approach are as convincing as they seem, then time should be made available for it to be an integral part of the curriculum for pupils with special needs.

An added incentive for pupils involved in a 'paired-reading' programme occurs if, at some stage, they are given the opportunity to 'tutor' younger pupils, say those in the first year. This approach of 'peer tutoring' has recently gained respectability through the work of Wheldall and Metten. It was found that 'low achieving' 16-year-olds trained to tutor reading using the 'pause, prompt and praise' method with 12-year-old 'remedial children who were retarded in reading' showed, at the end of the programme, a marked improvement in their own reading accuracy as a result of tutoring the younger pupils who also improved (Wheldall and Metten, 1985, p. 27).

Such accounts clearly demonstrate that difficulties in learning are bound up with the individual's lack of confidence and feelings of inadequacy. Lawrence (1973) recognised that the most outstanding characteristic of pupils' difficulty in reading was their poor emotional adjustment, and yet, its remedy so often takes the form of a direct attack on the mechanics of reading; rarely is there a systematic plan to care for the child's emotional state and self-image through counselling. This has again become a subject for discussion in a later paper by Lawrence (1985) entitled 'Improving self-esteem and reading'. Through convincing research findings, it was demonstrated how groups of pupils who received help with the skills or reading through Distar (Direct Instructional Teaching technique devised by Englemann, Osborn and Englemann, 1969) will show high gains in reading if this help is supplemented by a therapeutic approach aimed at enhancing self-esteem. The evidence suggests that teachers can be more effective in their efforts to help pupils with reading difficulties if, in some cases, they systematically pay attention to the pupil's self-concept. By supplementing the teaching of reading skills with a programme of either counselling or drama, the pupils could enhance self-esteem and also improve reading skills.

Familiarising oneself with the work of Rogers (1975) on the nature, value and establishment of empathy would help teachers towards an appreciation of the possibility that pupils who are failing in reading and seem to be avoiding it, could simply be behaving according to their perception of themselves. Self-concept, in part, is formed through a 'looking-glass' reflection of other people's perceptions. It can be inferred that the pupil's perceptions of themselves will change if the teacher is perceived as valuing her pupils more positively. Throughout Lawrence's research, a combination of humanistic and learning theory principles was attempted. The essence of such an approach lies in the quality of the relationship which sets out to be accepting and non-judgemental. An atmosphere of trust was established within which the children

felt free to confide. Lawrence (1973; 1985) has consistently emphasised that not all pupils seemed to need a therapeutic programme.
Such pupils are those whose reading failure is not associated with
any emotional problem. These are pupils who normally achieve
quick success with individual attention to their reading skills and
very soon, their confidence is restored. Lawrence (1985) suggested
that the sequence of action should be first to focus on the 'skill
approach' and then to look at 'within child factors' only if success is
not forthcoming after this first stage.

But are the views of Kohl (1974) and Lawrence (1973; 1985) now
being given practical application? Not so, judging from the
inspectorate:

> ... once fluency is achieved, assessment should be based on what
> pupils are actively reading for real interest and real purposes, rather
> than on exercise material. It is all too common to find that the progress
> of primary pupils is assessed by how far they have got through a
> graded reading scheme, rather than by understanding of and interest
> in material read for a purpose, for curiosity, or because it is enjoyable.
> It is all too common to find that the reading of junior and secondary
> pupils is assessed in terms of their ability to perform 'comprehension
> exercises' on out-of-context passages in text books or on work cards,
> rather than on their response to, say, the class reader, to newspaper
> and magazine articles, or to informational material, such as
> brochures, of the kind that they do or will need to use.
>
> (DES, 1984, p. 20)

The statement offers little in defence of a reading approach which
involves only following sequential reading schemes that are graded
and structured — those which leave very little opportunity for other
kinds of involvement with language through an enjoyment of
books. Forcing pupils to read for words, or worse still for syllables,
when they can already read for meaning, is insupportable. In such a
regime, there will have been little attempt to assemble books which
feed the imagination or challenge the young reader; books which
contain fairy stories, myths and legends: stories and poems which
have nothing to do with sequential reading structure, but everything to do with the business of growing up as real readers. If we
were as sensitive to the child and the story as we are receptive to
methods and structure materials, we might be set on a more hopeful
course.

What happens instead with pupils who find reading difficult is
that often, structured reading programmes are exclusively favoured
by teachers because the structure is an external prop, strengthening
our belief that pupils are making progress in a way that can be
measured objectively. It also serves to relieve us of the task of

sorting out why stories are important. If we are to select books which are worthwhile for our pupils, then we need to know what the reading of poetry and fiction entails; what is happening to the learner which makes the experience valuable. The test we should be applying is not Schonell, Burt, Daniels and Diack or Neale, but a simple quesiton: Is it worth reading? For reading to be an engagement which leads to imaginative control of texts, the reading of 'good' books must take priority over the superficial and threadbare reading schemes and kits so popular in many areas of 'compensatory' language curricula.

THE NEED TO READ

> The pattern, the idea, the ecstacy; it is for these that we must read, not for the word, the fact, the material out of which they are wrought.
> (T. Earle Welby, *The Dinner Knell*, 1932)

The questions of why books? and why literature at all? are ones which we as teachers of English take for granted simply by virtue of our own commitment to literature. One claim of literature is that it provides imaginative insight into what another person is feeling, and allows for the contemplation of possible human experiences which exist beyond the reader's daily awareness. Literature then, is a *vital need* which has the capacity, it is claimed, to develop empathy. That it is the experience of literature which promotes the education of the emotions is doubted by Gibble (1983) who argued that our emotional involvement rests solely at the mercy of the writer's art. While this cannot be denied, for pupils to be sensitive to this art, they first must have full emotional possession of a text for themselves and be brought into an encounter with language in its most complex and varied forms. A text is brought into existence by the active involvement of the reader. Though the writer is responsible for creating the story-world, it is the reader who has to shade in the outline, make the living connections and thus bring the text to life. Reading must be a personal engagement so that the reader 'lives through' the text as it happens.

One of the most convincing testimonies of this process can be found in the concluding volume of the autobiography of Simone de Beauvoir (1972). Here, she discloses remembrances of herself as an adolescent reader:

> When I was a child and an adolescent, reading was not only my favourite pastime, but also the key that opened the world to me. It foretold my future: I identified myself with the heroines of novels, and through them I caught glimpses of what my life would be. In the

unhappy phases of my youth it preserved me from loneliness; later it broadened my knowledge, increased my experience and helped me to a better understanding of my state as a human being and of the meaning of my work as a writer.

(Beauvoir, 1972, p. 157)

She goes on to admit how 'reading alone creates new and lasting relationships between things and myself' (Beauvoir, 1972, p. 159). Such joy and lasting delight needs little justification. How then, can we convince our pupils of this vital need and dare them to make the necessary leap of the imagination?

It is not particularly the shortage of adolescent fiction which presents the problems, nor is it the variety from which to choose (a browse through the 'Puffin Plus' series for example is sufficient evidence). Even though we vaguely and guiltily know there are plenty of books to interest and extend our pupils, often through limited time and resources, we become frightened into conservatism, training that kestrel year after year in a belief that for our lower-band pupils *Kes* remains the archetype (Hines, 1968). Not only will the textual demands of such books force us to look further when selecting material for our pupils, we are also trying to find ways of persuading them that reading isn't boring.

With classes where reading and the use of books is seen as a chore, the teacher will still be in quest of the class reader that 'works' with disaffected fourth- and fifth-year pupils. To form a close engagement between the child's private inner world and the creator of a text, does it necessarily follow that the child has to 'live through' a story in a book first? The teacher in the next example persuaded her class towards alternative ground through Barry Hines' film *Threads* which, having been filmed in their home city, had particular appeal for her pupils. Though the film's main concern was the social issue of nuclear war, and inevitably the pupil-talk included discussing the nuclear debate, the film was used primarily as an art form in itself and later as a means of encouraging the group towards a deeper understanding of stories such as Robert O'Brien's *Z for Zachariah* (O'Brien, 1976) and Bob Swindell's *Brother in the Land* (Swindell, 1984).

After watching the film *Threads* together as a class, smaller groups exchanged their views and in some cases their fears, of nuclear war:

Ian: What did you think about it?
Toni: I thought it were rare good.
Ann: Rare good? I thought it were good wi' t'explosion and that.

Ian:	What did you think about it John?
John:	It were good — but it frightens me a bit.
Ian:	Why's it frighten you?
John:	To think of dying — but if it were to happen I'd hope t'bomb lands on top of me.
Toni:	I-I-I wouldn't want-want to see what had happened afterwards. I'd rather just get killed.
Mark:	I'd just spend ten quid and get drunk.
Toni:	I bet!
Ian:	Do you fink — do you fink t'special effects were good — any good?
Mark:	Yeh.
Michael:	They were rare good.
Toni:	I-I thought that were good where they'd made t'Woolworths and that like.
Ian:	Yeh — brilliant that weren't it?
Toni:	Yeh — and I fought ...
Mark:	I'd be where it were going to land.
Ian:	John — if you survived — survived the bomb what would you do? Would you try ...
John:	I'd probably kill meself.
Ian:	Why?
John:	Cos I wouldn't like to live afterwards when there's nobody about hardly and then I'd die of radiation poisoning.
Ann:	And that when they had to eat that sheep.
Ian:	What would you do Toni?
Toni:	I'd get stoned.
Ian:	What would you do Mark?
Mark:	I'd probably get killed.

In re-living the film, the pupils admit their anxieties predicting their personal reactions in the event of a nuclear war. Their discussion is operating on another level however. Prompted mainly by Ian's question concerning 'special effects', the focus shifts so that the group consider the film as an art-form, itself worthy of comment. These two distinct levels of awareness continue to develop simultaneously throughout the pupils' talk. The pupils are no longer merely voyeurs of the screen drama but participants in the lives of real people for whose fate they have genuine concern:

Ann:	Did you see that woman holding her baby — and it had all one eye that was covered in blood and t'baby were ...
John:	Oh shut up!
Ann:	And that woman walked past — it was terrible.

Toni:	Yeh and it weren't very well an' all. There were lots of reight good parts in it warn't th'? It were right realistic.
Ian:	What did you think to the acting of it?
Toni:	I thought it were brilliant!
Ann:	Brilliant.
Toni:	They did it like it were real didn't they like?
Ian:	Yeh.
Ann:	Yeh.
Toni:	But it scares you dun't it?
Ann:	I hope none o' it never happens.
John:	If it does happen I'd prefer to die straight away.
Michael:	I'd rather just kill missen (myself) before that happened.
John:	What do you think about it Ian?
Ann:	I don't know how that woman had that baby after all she went through.
Toni:	I know — just think of t'baby — it could be scarred or summat like that. It could die of radiation.
Ian:	I think erm I'd rather live in a foreign country like South Africa where t'bombs er ...
Mark:	Not there — it showed you di'n't it — on that thing.
Ann:	I wonder when — I wonder whether them next door got out on t' county.
John:	Oh yeh them that were going to Lincoln to see t' ...
Ann:	Yeh.
John:	They.
Ian:	They all got shrivvled up.

The film was fast becoming for this group a 'text' within its own right creating for the pupils a sensitivity towards public issues which they themselves felt required urgent debate.

Ian:	Do you think they should ban nuclear weapons or ...
Ann:	Yeh.
Toni:	Yer.
John:	But they're thinking of starting it out in space though aren't they like Star Wars?
Ian:	Yea.
Toni:	If they're going to fight I don't know whey they just don't fair fight instead of dropping bombs and that.
Ann:	(in agreement) Mm ...
Mark:	It's too easy though in' it — nuclear bombs?
Ian:	Do you think Britain should have nuclear weapons?
Sam:	No.
John:	Yeh – yeh in a way 'cos ...

Michael:	Yes 'cos if they — if they …
Toni:	Yes 'cos if that country puts down theirs I don't see why we shouldn't put ours …
Ann:	That country — that country would have got more food if it weren't for all t'nuclear weapons.
Toni:	But what's point of all t'fighting anyway? Why don't they just stop fighting?
Ann:	Make peace.
Sam:	Yeh.
John:	And if it does come — nuclear war — nuclear war, why don't t'leaders fight it out — not us?
Toni:	Say like — say like if you had a nuclear bomb and they dropped theirs and we dropped ours and then it'd be like nob'dy living wun' it?
John:	Yeh.
Toni:	There's no point in it I don't think.
Ian:	Might as well just destroy t'earth.
Toni:	I know, there's no point in it it's just stupid!

The pupils' angry frustration at the futility of such a threat is evident, and at this point, the teacher considers that her group is receptive to learn how other people have similarly tried to make sense of this same problem through expressing their feelings in some tangible art-form: visual material such as *Atom Piece* by Henry Moore was incorporated alongside poems of a similar theme — Miroslav Holub's *The Forest* ; Angela M. Clifton's *Hiroshima*; Adrian Mitchell's *Appendix IV*; James Kirkup's *No More Hiroshima's*. These were supplemented by a more familiar but dependable favourite Peter Porter's *'Your Attention Please'*: it must surely have become standard practice for this particular poem to be pre-recorded on cassette tape, letting the narrative interrupt perhaps a current pop-music programme as a 'newsflash'; the startling effect never fails initially to con and then to captivate even the most unlikely listener.

Just as the group were able to assess the artistic merit of the film *Threads*, so they displayed equal confidence when discussing the language of these poems:

Ann:	(Refers to poem and reads aloud) 'The bomb burst like a flower'. Why did it burst like a flower?
Mark:	Because it was growing up in the sky.
Ann:	Because what?
Mark:	It was growing up into the sky.
Ann:	No — it might be because t'sky was opening out quick like the bomb.

Samantha:	Spread and …
Richard:	What — like a mushroom?
Ann:	Yeh.
Mark:	Ever — everyone afterwards thought it were — thought it were like smoke from an industrial chimney — but really it were — were like a nuclear bomb.
Richard:	I don't think so. I think it's — er — a bit more.
Ann:	Er …
Richard:	They must have thought it were a big bomb them people.
Ann:	It says 'and men stood afar off and …' How can they … — erm — how can they stand theer when t'bomb's … bomb's gone off?
Richard:	Don't know.
Ann:	It says 'The bomb burst like a flower/And grew upwards under the sun'.
John:	Mebbe it were …
Richard:	They were far away on t'hills and that were up in t' valley — in the city and they was — just around it.
Ann:	I know but wun't (wouldn't) it still ger 'em?
Mark:	Yeh.
Richard:	Well yeh, it'd get 'em later.
Mark:	It'd drift away towards 'em.
Ann:	Then why are they still stood theer then?
Mark:	They don't know what it is an' it's first time they've seen a nuclear bomb.
Richard:	And it looks cruel (pause). You know *Threads*?
Ann:	Yeh.
Richard:	When they — erm — turned and saw the cloud going up.
Ann:	Yeh.
John:	It were a big flower.
Richard:	Well that's what it meant about these men looking up and wondering what it is — 'cos they didn't know anything about a nuclear attack.
Ann:	Do you know anything about one?
Richard:	Only that I don't want to get blown up!

Ann's initial puzzlement over the poet's choice of simile 'Why did it burst like a flower?' invites the group to comment. Immediately an engagement with the text is formed in the way that the collective response subtly echoes the imagery of the poem: phrases such as 'growing up in the sky'; 'opening out'; 'spread' and 'like a mushroom' suggest an almost intuitive understanding of the poem.

A further attempt to make sense of the poem is implicit in the way Mark makes a comparison between the nuclear bomb — which is outside his immediate experience — with something tangible ' like smoke from an industrial chimney' which he draws from his known experience; he thus puts the language of the poem within the context of his own understanding.

Still finding the poem illogical, Ann poses another vexed question: 'how can they stand theer when t'bombs — bomb's gone off?' Between them Mark and Richard rely upon a sustained visual impact of the film *Threads* to illustrate their hypothesis. They gently coax Ann to remember the group's shared experience of watching the film — 'You know *Threads*?' — gradually persuading her towards an understanding of the text.

Such involvement in the texture of words is evident in Mark's 'It'd drift towards 'em', Richard's 'And it looks cruel' and John's approximation of the poem's imagery 'it were a big flower'. Such rich verbal expression is ratified in later written responses:

> The warning is alerted
> The cloud floats up
> All humanity petrified
> All humanity desolate
> Life no more.
> > Des (aged 14)

For Des to produce merely five lines after being immersed in hours of carefully chosen film and poetry may be justifiably unacceptable — at the very least disheartening — to the teacher, but she is aware that it represents much painstaking labour for this pupil. With clipped cinematographic style, Des economically suggests a possible sequence of events in a nuclear holocaust: the simplicity of the response is its strength as it strains to gain a climax by the last line.

An attempt by Toni, on the other hand, at once pitches us straight amid the panic and confusion as the bomb explodes:

> The warning is given
> People shout and run for help
> They run from the mushroom in the sky
> The heat is amazing and people die
> But the survivors have to face the winter
> Where the fall-out lands upon them
> And people begin to think they should have died.
> > Toni (aged 14)

According to Toni, it is the survivors, not the dead, who are to be pitied, as they are the ones left to contend with the blight of the nuclear winter. Of the pieces received from this group, Michael's is perhaps the one which best illustrates the need for the careful selection of literature as starting points for the pupils' own written responses:

> *The Nuclear Bomb*
> The bomb looks like a mushroom
> And it burst like a flower
> The Clour where grey and orange. (colours were)
> But soon a snowstorm of radio
> active fall-out
>   blow across the land and
> It could kill everybody.

From poems already presented to him in class, Michael directly lifts two lines which he uses initially. These lines act as pegs from which he hangs his own language until he feels confident enough to make that creative leap towards constructing his personal images. The point at which this happens is discerned when Michael sacrifices technical accuracy to his more immediate task of image-making. So delicate is this process that the teacher has to resist all intervention for the purpose of correcting errors until she receives Michael's offering: only then dare she suggest how to create a more public version.

> The bomb looks like a mushroom
> And it bursts like a flower
> The colours were grey and orange.
> But soon a snowstorm of radio-active fall-out
> Blows across the land, and
> It could kill everybody.
>   Michael (aged 14)

Very little redrafting was required for this piece from Donna:

> The first thing we know
> Is the mushroom-shaped cloud
> The bright light hurting our eyes.
>
> Even years and years later
> Our children would feel the pain
> They will still feel the cold.
>
> The red.

> The big mushroom in the sky
> The white heat and blast
> The red sky.
> Like a clown blowing up a
> Balloon in a circus.
> That was fun.
> This is not.
>
> After all the pain
> Nobody can win.
> Because there's nobody
> Left to win over
> Even the people who
> Set it off
> Are gone.
> So what's the point?
> > Donna (aged 14)

Donna handles the language with confidence and her central comparison which likens the bomb-blast to 'a clown blowing up a balloon in a circus' is entirely her own. Through a series of carefully balanced associations, the poem protests against the futility of nuclear war; and together with Donna's skilful use of subtle emphasis and varied rhythm we are prepared for the final rhetorical question: 'What's the point?'

With groups where the book has in the past, failed to captivate them, the 'film to book' approach is usually successful, especially sure winners such as *Gregory's Girl* by Kenneth Cole (Cole, 1981), *The Ghost in the Water* by Edward Chitham (Chitham, 1982) or those serialised on television — among them *Buddy* by Nigel Hinton (Hinton, 1982); *Carrie's War* by Nina Bawden (Bawden, 1973) or Robert Westall's *The Machine Gunners* (Westall, 1975). Because a certain novel may pose textual difficulties for pupils with special needs, the film version need not be ignored. Examples in this category would include Fowles' *The French Lieutenant's Woman*; Hardy's *Far From the Madding Crowd*; Emily Brontë's *Wuthering Heights*; Orwell's *1984* and even the most truculent pupils find some attraction to Roman Polanski's adaptation of *Romeo and Juliet*. The film will not substitute for the book, both are different art-forms which are worthy of independent study, but film does supplement lively story-making. In such a context, pupils will be encouraged to form an active engagement with texts through keeping reading journals, writing interventions to the story, improvisation and role-play, interviewing characters and making videos of scenes.

Once they experience 'storying' as a pleasurable activity, pupils with special needs can be encouraged to talk about the reading

process as they experience it, rather than expected to produce
written responses. Protherough (1983) in his book *Developing
Response to Fiction* identified five distinct modes of response:
projection into a character; projection into the situation; associating
between book and reader; the distanced viewer and detached
evaluation. In the next transcript, Pat, when questioned about what
happens when she reads, had this to say:

Teacher: And what er — when you're reading a book — what
            happens in your imagination? Do you actually —
Pat: I imagine it's me.
Teacher: You imagine it's you — good.

Pat was revealing how she became the character of the book and
demonstrated a conscious awareness of her active imagination by
describing her ability to 'lose herself' in the character's personality
and situation. Within small group discussion, Pat then goes on to
discuss the value of books without pictures:

Pat: Don't you like long stories wi'aht t' pictures?
Andrea: No, they're boring then ...
Pat: Cos you can't read 'em?
Andrea: ... I can read books but I can't read long stories.
Pat: You prefer reading pictures.
Andrea: Yeh.
Pat: It sounds daft but you do. What do you like reading
            Maria?
Maria: Me?
Pat: Yeh.
Maria: Oh that's interesting
Pat: Do you read just writing or ones wi' t'pictures?
Maria: One with pictures.
Pat: (to Andrea) which do you read?
Andrea: Both.
Pat: Which do you prefer?
Andrea: One wi' no pictures.
Pat: I do. You can get more into them.
Maria: Oh I don't.
Andrea: If they have no pictures in you can imagine what they're
            doing.
Pat: Yeh — you've got your own imagination to work on.

The girls in this group generally feel they can identify more with the
story if pictures are not present. Then, they can make their own
imaginative leap into texts and are able to 'live' through the story. In

the next sequence, these pupils are consciously aware that they have developed a keen interest for books which was not apparent at the beginning of their English course:

Pat: What books do you enjoy reading?
Maria: I don't read any. I pick one up, read t' first page and put it down. I can't remember what's happened. (Rachel laughs)
Pat: I used to be like that ...
Rachel: I did an' all.
Pat: ... but since Christmas, I've read about twenty books and I'm starting on that *Starting Over*. Then I read *Devil in Command* I carried on from theer (there).
Maria: Can't read long 'uns.
Pat: That's reason why you want to read 'em isn't it?
Maria: Like Andrea?
Andrea: You know since t'fifth year, I've read a load of books.
Pat: You know ...
Andrea: I never used to read.
Pat: That's what I thought other day. I was telling Michelle. I went into t'library the other day and I was looking for some right good books but I didn't know one author. I wanted to look for a good book and I though it's a bit bad in it, fifteen, nearly sixteen, and you don't know any.

There is evidence here, that the group is taking a more active part in learning. After experiencing the pleasure of reading, Pat for example, avidly reads everything at her disposal in the classroom library boxes. She is then motivated even further towards visiting the school library until finally, she ventures into the Public Library.

Pat: I was looking for a Catherine Cookson but they don't have her in t' central library. I couldn't find any anyway. There were the only ones. I didn't know any. So — It's a bit bad in it? (Pause) Have you read that what-the-call-it? *Twelfth of July*?
Maria: Me mother's read it.
Pat: It's good that. I like it — wish they were more like it.

There is little doubt that the pupils' new awareness of books will force them to seek familiarisation with authors and sequels to books already enjoyed, such as those by Joan Lingard (Lingard, 1970) which Pat hinted at.

Behind such new enthusiasm, the teacher's own imaginative engagement will involve her not only looking for fresh ways of working with texts, but also in more large-scale projects, such as inviting writers into school to talk about their work, setting up class libraries, school book clubs and book events, and inviting authors in, so that the reading environment is one that will encourage active readers in the fullest sense.

Must it always be books?

It has been shown how the 'text' of English Studies need not necessarily mean that fiction, in the form of novels or short-stories has to be used first. With pupils who are experiencing learning difficulties associated with language, it often helps to remove learning from the confines of the classroom to find ways that friends can share knowledge and to build from everyday experiences which enter the classroom (see Walsh (1983) for a more detailed development of this view).

Working thus from an awareness of her pupils' needs involves the teacher in patterning work around a pupil's particular experience. Such opportunities to be shared may be relatively spontaneous or even seasonal (isn't Keats' ode more fully appreciated in the autumn term?); other more individual experiences may take longer to be realised. Throughout the incubation, the teacher's role is that of 'imaginative opportunist' who uses accidental happenings to match up the right book or poem with a revealed interest at the appropriate time. This does not imply becoming hidebound by motorbikes, soccer or pop — though such social culture may well contribute to the overall pattern — rather through empathetic listening and close observation, the teacher can discern recurring emotional patterns of preoccupation and interest in the pupil to which English Studies can become satisfyingly in tune. In so doing, the pupils' unique ways of seeing themselves and the world around them and how that perception develops in response to the changing worlds of home and school, will be given the attention it deserves.

What follows is an illustration of how an unplanned opportunity was developed to serve the more long-term need of individual pupils. It is the first day back at school after the summer vacation and both teacher and pupils are engaged in discussing the highs and lows of their respective holidays. Katrina is somewhat subdued but the reason becomes apparent as the following extract from the teacher's journal evidences:

7th September
Katrina told me that she was due to go to the police station on Saturday morning after she had been arrested for shoplifting from a local department store. This disclosure encouraged Jimmy and Nigel to talk openly about similar experiences when they had 'nicked things' from shops during a day-trip to the coast. This is something that needs to be explored perhaps through role-play.

We've chosen to read together Nigel Hinton's *Collision Course*, which is quite an apt decision in the light of our discussion; it will also connect with Andrew's and Rachel's interest in motorbikes.

These shared experiences were to anticipate a later more public event which was similarly documented:

30th September
It is a fortunate coincidence that the Local Chamber of Trade have sent circulars round to schools in order to highlight the increase of shoplifting incidents involving pupils under 16. A competition is being run aimed to make this age-group more aware of the severity of such crimes. In view of previous admissions, it would seem appropriate to encourage the group to enter this competition. There could be collaboration with the Art Department here as an essay has to be accompanied with a painted poster entitled 'Stop Thief'.

As a starting point we read a playscript from David Walker's *Dilemmas* (Walker, 1979); the particular script 'I'll Take it Back' tells of a girl who, jealous of her friend's apparent affluence, steals a cassette tape from her. Once the playscript had been read, several of the group went to record their comments about shoplifting. Andrew began to write a poem while others tried a more sustained piece of writing. Amien, who can never sit still, wandered out to the side of me and picked up my copy of *Joby* (Stan Barstow) which I had earlier marked at the passages concerning the shoplifting episodes. 'It's great this book!' he enthusiastically declared, 'I'm going to the back of the class to read it.' He was next accompanied by John and Jimmy who began to read aloud in turn to each other.

While not the most imaginative choice of titles nowadays (Nigel Hinton's *Buddy* (Hinton, 1982) would have been better), *Joby* (Barstow, 1964) nevertheless re-kindled in Amien sparks of recognition from earlier pleasant associations with a story. This particular book provides both an immediacy of social realism for the whole group, and an emotional focus for individuals such as Amien whose engagement stems from deeper roots of feeling embedded in the text. Using the resources available to her at the time, the teacher seizes the opportunity to help pupils explore earlier lived moments of experience while simultaneously attending to their present needs. They are given further encouragement to articulate their experiences which are captured in the subsequent discussion:

Amien: Right! Come on then, Jimmy, tell us about the time that you went shoplifting.
Jimmy: Me?
Amien: Yeh ... talk sensible.
John: Sh ...

Jimmy:	Well I were wi' Bowler — reight? An' we got ont' bus going down town for his muvver.
Amien:	Speak up !
Jimmy:	Well we got on to' bus and found this quid, so we picked it up. You know that GT Stores where we went to Murbooshie? at the top of the road? Well that one.
Amien:	Aye.
Jimmy:	That one. So we goes walking in and he gets his things and I look o'er towards t' counter and no-one were there so I picks up a 'Mars Bar' and put it in me pocket. And I picks up another and walks off wi' it in me pocket. I picked up a 'Marathon' as well. And Bowler goes 'Ye Jammy bastard' (laughs).
John:	Nah den Amien, have you ever got caught shoplifting?
Amien:	Nah! I got taken to West Bar Police Station 'cos me mate did though. Gi-oor Pemberton! Off dem books! Get out Pemberton! You can't have it!
John:	And what happened when you got took down to West Bar?
Amien:	They kept me in t'Police Station for six hours.
Jimmy:	In di what?
Amien:	In the Police Station for about six hours.
Jimmy:	Honest? Did they nab you?
Amien:	An' me muvver had to come down and she took t'fit and I had to go and give a statement and she smacked me on t'eead (head) wi' 'andbag!
John:	Have you ever been shoplifting Andrew?
Andrew:	Yeh!
Amien:	Aye — he nicked dem pens didn't you?
John:	Tell us about what tha nicked.
Andrew:	Haven't nicked owt!
John:	What about … what about that metal plate thing what you nicked wi' someone's name on it?
Andrew:	Ooh!
John:	Gi-oor (next follows some inaudible talk) Come on! You're supposed to be talking about thieving — not messing about.

This conversation is ironically 'honest'. With small group talk such as this, there is more meaningful activity going on at a simple noisy level than we often realise until we repeatedly listen to the taped discourse. In this conversation for example, much anecdotal information is being exchanged and explored. As a result, relationships become more personal during which more incidents are revealed and, evident in the use of the present tense, are re-lived.

The spoken utterence has become the medium for expression of feelings and for making sense of the lived world. We have now all become participants in this re-lived experience which is brought graphically, and at times amusingly before us. We cannot ignore Jimmy's unconscious lapse into the present tense as he re-enacts his experience; neither can we avoid feeling Amien's embarrassment when, for all his vaunted display of courage, he cannot avoid his mother's wrath as she smacked him 'on t'eead wi' 'andbag'.

So what appears to be a mere engagement in ordinary conversation is really an enhancement of *living in* another human being. Only when we begin to recognise this can we begin to appreciate what the pupil has to say in terms of human values, in what Leavis has termed a 'criss-cross of utterance' between us. Similarly, Lomas (1981) stressed that there must be this 'ordinariness of language' if we are to encourage meaningful relationships between human beings. He goes so far as to say that the nearer we stay to 'common speech' the less likely we are to destroy the meaning of those who seek our help. Talk then should be the nucleus of learning through which there is an engagement of the person, of things and in others. Language begins with human reality which finds in communication through talk, a mode of self affirmation and establishment in the world. Helping learners to discover their innermost needs through talk and the allied narrative arts, is thus seen to be the initial stage by which a teacher is to engage the child in learning. Further more, spoken anecdotes can often be transformed by the pupil into the more self-disclosed formalised medium of writing as the next chapter describes.

From Katrina's first disclosure that she was 'up for shoplifting' it would have been only too easy for the teacher–pupil defences to harden into moralising: instead, the whole group became engaged in deciding what constituted their immediate and long-term needs. When lived moments such as these are allowed to become shared experiences teacher and pupil offer each other the reality of their ordinary warmth and understanding towards an acceptance of each other — their fundamental need.

SUMMARY

This chapter explored various aspects of the narrative arts and discussed their necessity to English studies. Alternative approaches to reading have been suggested for those pupils for whom more traditional methods have little effect. The 'film of the book' has always been a useful standby as a speedy way of getting through a set text. It was demonstrated how film can be used as a way of actually getting into the novel through the considerations of how both texts relate the same narrative, producing meanings in the languages that they have at their disposal.

Communication Through Writing

> But it is only human nature to put your heart into what you write and
> say how you feel.
>
> (Majella: aged 15)

Partly due to the artificiality of the task, writing is something which
pupils with special needs often find particularly difficult. Part of
their problem however, could rest with the type of written work
they are expected to endure. When encouraged to produce
continuous pieces of writing, it is not uncommon for the class
teacher to notice how during a lesson, some individuals never seem
to progress beyond a 'pen-chewing stage'; the only tangible
evidence of their effort will be their name and the date written at the
top of the page followed by the almost obligatory 'One day me
and ... '. Equally, but displaying their frustration more forcibly, are
those individuals who screw up or tear up their meagre efforts,
scribble over it, or more damagingly, destroy the work of the pupil
sitting next to them. We recall again Tom Brangwen's frustration
with writing:

> Then he reddened furiously, felt his bowels sink with shame,
> scratched out what he had written, made an agonised effort to think
> of something in the real composition style. Failed, became sullen with
> rage and humiliation, put the pen down, and would have been torn to
> pieces rather than attempt to write another word.
>
> (D. H. Lawrence (1915) *The Rainbow*. Chapter 1, p. 17)

This passage parallels the plight of a fifth former, David, who tore
his work up into small pieces after declaring to his class teacher
'I'm no good at this me'. The following extract from the teacher's
journal describes the event:

> *10th March*
> David is amazing. He is still so embarrassed with his work that he tore
> up one of the chronically few pieces of writing from his file. I emptied
> the waste-paper basket at the end of the lesson to retrieve his writing.
> After this, I spent two hours piecing together the jig-saw, sticking it
> and having it photocopied.

The piece of writing which the teacher reconstituted read as
follows:

A Night Out

The last time I had a night out I went to a youth club I went to see
whote it was like I got to the club then I went to the door then I went to
the pay box I sed to her how much is it she sed to me it is fivpence.
And then she sed to me whote is your name I told her and then she
told me my number of the club the number was 54. then I went a way
whith my pals and I sed to my pals whote is the games in here they
sed to me they is snooker and tabltenis or football and whitelifting
and all sor they is spaceinverdors and all sor they is pool game played
one of my meats sed to me whode you like to play tabletenis I said to
him I play you then he went to the play desk to get the table tenis set
he brout it down onto the table then the game when on them five
minets whent them the laby on the pay desk shouted to us your game
is up then we packed to the game up them we tuck it back to the pay
box. then when we finist my meat sed to me would you like to play
snooker I sed to him I witill play you he got the game from the pay box
we set the game up then we plade.

For many pupils then, the pen becomes an instrument of torture. At
the same time, the class teacher dare not allow too many
temperamental outbursts from her pupils so as a compromise, it is
all too easy to expect the class to put up with mostly dull, mechanical
exercises aimed to improve their skills of punctuation and spelling,
while at the same time, subduing the pupils' fundamental need to
express themselves. Similar observations have been made by
Barnes and Barnes (1984) and by Gordon and Wilcox (1983) who are
concerned that children with special needs devote too much time to
improving a narrow range of ill-defined skills. It is hardly surprising
therefore, that when pupils have been brought up with such an
arid regime, they find it difficult to develop more mature forms
of writing which depend on the ordered distilling of experience
through careful drafting and re-drafting processes. The following
work from Andrew serves to illustrate this point. His first draft
produced:

> crouel
> fast movemets
> fear withn
> clear
> (furtive) glance
> selling for profet

The Shoplifter

The shoplifter a crouel member of the comunity
the fast movemets of his hands Baffle
the Police until numnes nearly sets in there
feable Brains.

One is at once puzzled by Andrew's use of the word 'crouel' (cruel) when writing about a shoplifter until he explained that he wanted to say that shoplifters are selfish and 'cruel members of the society'. He goes on in line 2 to describe the deftness of the shoplifter and in line 3 makes a comment upon the fear experienced by the criminal. It was when he reached lines 4 and 5 that Andrew encountering his first difficulty asks the teacher for help:

Andrew: I want to put that he looked over his shoulder like that. (Here he demonstrates by looking over his own shoulder.) And he looks to see if anyone is watching him ... out of the corner of his eye.

Teacher: There is a word you could use here — it's 'furtive' meaning a bit sly, cautious ...

Andrew: Yeh! That's it — furtive!

Teacher: Okay ... He makes a 'furtive glance'. (Here the teacher writes down the new word for Andrew.) Now carry on writing down a few more ideas — then add a bit more detail.

Andrew's final line conveys an idea that the shoplifter would 'sell for profit'.

By the second draft, Andrew has already put a title, written more detail in his second and third lines and introduces a further dimension 'numnes nearly sets in there feable brains'. An attempt is now being made to shape further the material from Andrew's first jottings. It is a conscious phase during which the teacher, while watching the pattern unfolding, is readily available to offer support when help is needed.

The process is often repeated time and time again until the near 'final draft' emerges from the cocoon of feelings, observations and associations. As the pupils re-draft their work they are moving from private to public worlds. They are not bored with writing because now they have something they want to communicate.

The chore of re-drafting can be minimised even further by using a word-processor with a programme such as 'Wordwise', 'Write' or 'Pen Down'. When the learner is accused of being 'a poor speller' and 'hopeless at punctuation' could we similarly accuse ourselves of not looking beyond the mistakes to find the meaning of what the pupil is struggling to say?

From the near final draft (see over) it was obvious that there was still some ambiguity, but before this was shaped further, the teacher asks Andrew to show that he understood his own written response, to evaluate it himself. The teacher does this by inviting Andrew's comments on some of the more obscure phrases:

Teacher: Right Andrew, tell me what you meant when you said that the shoplifter is a 'cruel member of the community'?

Andrew: Well he didn't think about other people's feelings.

Teacher: Mmm.

Andrew: He just thought about money — taking things from other people.

Teacher: Yes ... and why 'numbness nearly sets in their feeble brains'?

Andrew: Well they don't use their brains — they take it out of spite or whatever (pause).

Teacher: And what's this 'furtive glance'?

Andrew: I don't know, you said that ... (pause) ... (cough) ... it's er checkin' round in't it?

Teacher: Mmm.

Andrew: To see if anyone is looking at them like detectives.

Teacher: What kind of a glance is a furtive glance then ...

Andrew: Secret ... or slyly.

Teacher: Secret or sly. Good! Then what does it — what tone of voice did you want to have down here (points to end of poem) 'You must have your little extra luxuries'? What were you thinking and feeling behind that?

Andrew: I don't know.

Teacher: Can you say anything about this Amien? Have you read it?

Amien: Yeh — it's about some people they rob just for the sake on it. Some people rob when they need it, but some when they're not needing it.

Teacher: Mmm ... You've put the shoplifter 'Does not seem to have thought of the consequences'. Now what does the consequences of shoplifting involve? What are the consequences? What consequences?

Amien: Get caught!

Andrew: Prison ... Borstal.

Teacher: Fines?

Amien: Showing up. Yeh it's put in t'paper when you're caught shoplifiting.

Teacher: That's it. Good ... so — when you were actually writing this did you have a picture of someone actually doing this — in your mind — what things did you actually feel when you were writing it?

Andrew: No I just thought about shoplifting and thought about what a shoplifter would do.

Teacher: Right ... good! Thanks very much.

Through this particular discourse, language is seen to have the function for the participants 'of making explicit to themselves — as much as to other people, the nature of an insight already partly intuited' (Barnes, Briton and Rosen, 1969). Andrew's poem was under scrutiny from a wider audience of both the teacher and a friend — 'Can you say anything about this Amien. Have you read it?' The fragmented jigsaw of a poem is now complete and the final version reads as follows:

> Shoplifter ...
> Cruel member of the community
> Fast movements of his hands
> Baffle the Police until
> numbness
> nearly sets in their feeble brains.
>
> Fear is within them
> As they strike
> Hearts pound! and
> A furtive glance
> reassures them of their apparent
> innocence.
>
> What can you hope to gain?
> An extra watch?
> A pen?
> A ring or two
> Things you can really do without.
> But you *must* have your little extra luxuries.
>
> The shoplifter
> Seems not to have thought
> Of the consequences if he is caught for
> a little thing.
> Much more blame could be put on the
> man who takes for a laugh,
> or for some money
> on the side.
>
> (Andrew: aged 15)

Always working from the sense of the individual's special need, the teacher, as a starting point, tries to encourage her pupils to write one vignette of experience in the form of a short paragraph or poem. It is then easier for them to keep within the limits of their own technical ability in respect of vocabulary, spelling, syntax, handwriting and overall length. In this way, as much complexity of feeling as possible about the experience is concentrated into the writing. Adopting this approach does not lessen the fact that during the early stages a teacher will receive writing from the individual where spelling may be erratic to say the least; but in the event there can be concrete improvement here, because there is something that now awaits editing — which should be more meaningful a task than mechanical exercises allow. The following attempt from Darren, a third-year pupil from a mixed-ability group, shows that if the teacher would only look beyond the spelling mistakes she may find that her pupils are struggling to say something with greater expression than their attempts substantiate on first glance. This attempt was Darren's written response to *The Fight*, a poem by Gareth Owen, and the Lowry painting of the same title:

The Fight

The blood seeking spectators made an opening wich we went througg. It seemed to strach for ever. When we arived seming by at the center, my iner fealing not to fight, drained my currage so greatly, I felt I could hardly stand, as if I was sway-ing like a blade of grass in the wind and he — the graet oak sood high sturdy and all powerful, wored not while I was shaking feroisely I felt any moment I would die a death so shameful that I could only be glad I was dead.

He threw the first punch. I never saw it come, but I knew it arived right on the jaw. I felt dizzy so verey dizzy. Then came another one right in the stomach — so glad I was that I had had no tea. I went down. I could hardly breath. I got up and I threw punches in to the air I colapsed in a frensic state. I new the futile batal was over.

I didn't realy care. The crowed scatured and I heared one voice. It brought only fear. I wish I could have said, 'Beam me up Scotty', but I couldn't. What could I say that would cool my mum's nerves?
'danial, danial,' it bellowed.
'Where are you.'
'danial danial it's time for breackfast. I arowsed
It was a dream only a ferosias dream.

(Darren: aged 13)

In his second piece, Darren has developed his sensitivity to detail and while there is still difficulty with spelling, he does not allow it to frustrate his effort:

Winter Countryside

as distant tree's stand naked and tall on the horizon, a small delecate snow flake brushes past the face of a young rabbitt. shivering and alowne, on it hops into the wilderness.

Its foot prints split the hillside and indeed the night, as the cold frost bites its nose it rushes off quick now with more haste and fear as night is soon upon it. and as footprints in the snow are easy pray for Passing foxes.

> The snow falls hevier now and the wind is rising. The winter night playing with lonley, scared rabbit as it hurryies on it way a-lone, an owl breaks in the silance of the wind as the rabbit slips into a snow drifft as the snow flys and the wind howls the young rabbit gives up.
>
> He curls up and leaves only a nose, and two pink eyes to break the fur line as he looks out again, he notices a bush of green holy with rosy red berryies breaking trough the cold greys of the night.
>
> As stars apear in the deep blue sky the snow stops and clowds break. The light of the stars, so pure and birght illuminate the hill side an comfort the tired lonley rabit. who realises he is not alone. for in the distance moving with grace and power a young fox stalks the sine of the passing rabbit, slowly onward he strides and gracefully forward.
>
> The young rabit now see's that he is truly alone. his mather would have chased around in a frenze laying traks every where then quickly they would run off together into the night. But no, he did not have the energy nor courage.

It is not difficult to see why Darren had for some time, been labelled as 'dyslexic' by his teachers. The fear of spelling and punctuation errors had paralysed his written responses until he had been fully assured that once he had something meaningful to write, spellings and so on would eventually 'look after themselves'.

A similar lack of confidence in writing can be found in Gregory's attempts. In an early piece, written as a fourth-year pupil in a mixed-ability group, Gregory scribbled across his sheet. Some of his words are hard to decipher but this is what he wrote after the class were working round the theme of birth:

> The baby was in its cot swing rocking
> It's face was white as snow like a borof sope
> The baby was rapped up it soft nited blankits
> The dumy was a little round spek in the
> Baby's moth.

Looking beyond the difficult spellings, Gregory is showing evidence of symbol-making in the way he describes the baby's face being 'white as snow like a borof sope' and that 'the dumy was a little round spek' in the 'moth' (mouth) of the baby.

A later worksheet from Gregory shows similar bewilderment, though amid the crossings out and spelling errors can be found fresh images such as, 'the wind was ploughing' and 'the leves were sloly dripping off the ortem trees'. He writes also that 'the cristale sun was glowing down on the rippling sea'. Later he wrote this piece:

The Lightning Sky
It was an ugerlayday the cowdes was driping down on the world. It had just finished raining and the sun was creping throught the clowdes. I just put my £1.99 brolay. When it broke out lashing it down with a cool heule like me then all off a sudden the trees cret and crak and suddenly fell to the growened.

The heaviness of an impending storm is quite lucidly conveyed in Gregory's opening sentence 'it was a ugerlayday the cowdes was driping down on the world'. He personifies the sun 'creping throught the clowdes' and captures the onomatopoeic quality of 'the trees cret and crak and suddenly fell to the growened'.

In his struggle to produce his images, Gregory demonstrates the beginnings of a fresh awareness to his world, but these pieces were ones done merely to 'please the teacher' for it is early in the learning relationship and as yet, she is not aware of Gregory's real need nor of what he would personally like to express. He was later involved in a not too serious motorbike accident which resulted in him missing time from school; the teacher, on Gregory's return, used this to begin the art-making process (Abbs, 1982). However, this time the teacher encouraged Gregory to talk about his interest rather than to write about it:

The main thing about cleaning bikes is the engine... You should always clean the engine thoroughly and well 'cos if you go round t'track, chain might come off or might hit — or yuh might have a bad accident so — always clean yer bike well... The best part of the bike is when you're riding down t'field and yer burning Miss Calsh's War — Miss Walsh's Car 'bout 65–70 miles an hour (pause) an' (pause) mek sure you've allus got protective clothing an don't guh daft on t'bikes — 'cos when yer going round t'field yer could be riding along and you could hit summat an' yer could easily fall off so mek sure you've got protective clothing on. An another thing — be seen even if yer are in t'light. So Good Luck Riders! ... As I've just said be seen — don't be seen 'cos police might get yer ... You should always check your check your brakes clutch gears and etcetera because if you're going down a hill about 60 miles an hour or a little less you may have to do an emergency stop 'cos a rat or something might jump out in front of you, or something else or ... All my uvver friends have got bikes an' they keep theirs clean aswell so I will keep mine clean. My bruvver has got a bike a CCM Crosser 250 mine's a DT Induro motocross 100 and its not geared down like trial bikes. There is a difference between Motocross and Trials. Motocross is when you go round a big track going over big hills and bumps and Trialsing is when you is where your're going slowing doing all obstacles and things like that — it's been on telly so I'd rather do motocrossing myself — me friends would an' all — they don't like trialsing — they like it a bit but not alot ... You should always check your tyres and anything else 'cos if they'd got a puncture — a slow puncture you might not know it an' you might go down the field — and you could easily get — could easily get another puncture and it will go down even faster — and you don't like pushing bikes do you lads? (Gregory deepens the tone of his voice and speaks 'in role') No we don't.

I have got a red seat all — all my bike is red so I like the colour red ... I do all my own repairing even — but it anything else guz up with it very big my dad does it or if he can't do it he teks 'im (him) to the garage an' let the workmen do it so it waint (won't) get ruined. Nuffin' much guz up wi it because I keep it in very good condition ... I have got good protective clothes an' helmet. My helmet cost quite a bit. Best to have a good helmet than a likkle crap helmet because if — if you got an helmet that's been painted on it will crack easy but if you've got a brand new one that is so strong that not alot of thinks can break it ... You should always oil your bikes frequently an' well an' check the chain is tight ... That is the end of my report from Gregory Carroll. 4R. Miss Walsh.

Gregory shows a confidence through talk that is not evident in his writing. This example demonstrates a sense of audience as he seems to be addressing his listeners and at one stage begins, through role-play, re-creating. Much of the discourse is reflective, indicated by phrases such as 'yuh might have a bad accident', 'yer coud be riding along and you could hit summat an' you could easily fall off' and 'a rat or something might jump out in front of you' or regarding a slow puncture 'you might not know it an' you might go down the field — and you could easily get — could easily get another puncture'.

Though Gregory was willing and confident to talk about his experiences, he did not at that time have the same confidence in his writing. After he had given the opportunity to reveal his interests through talk, however, the impulse to write became stronger, as this next piece demonstrated.

My A+ day and My D− day

The best day had was when I got my motorbike. I had to klen it all up like a now bick. Then I stared to take all the part off to klen them indviduerlay. After I had klened them I put the bieck back to gether.

My A+ day

I rember when I got by bick whent out on the fieldis with my meat we was going along the fields with pete on the back and there was a big bumhole (bombhole) in the flour then and I hit a krak and we wnt fling in to the bumhole and in the hole there was a fencs and we went fling thoroght the fencs and we tumbled and roaied on to some concrete and we both fell of. We was laying on the floure and my neo felt a bit founy so I look at it and the was a big kut on my nee. Sundley I started to panic I did'tn now what to do then I ran up home them My stepmum rang up the hoslple and a ambulances come allso a police car as well to aske what happed and I sead that I fell of my bick. Then like a flash I was laying on the opurating table to be sticked up They sticked me up and put me a big bandig on my leg from my toe to my hip. I had 11 stickers in my nee then I was at home for a long time alway from school.

My D− day

Shortly after this, Gregory wanted to write about his bike and produced the following:

My Motorbike

I got my first bike when I was 8 it was only a small one and not powerfull. I got it seconed had. I used to clen it every day and if anything went wroting with it I used to mened it my self but if it was a big probulm My dad used to mened it. I had a yellow tank with some sticer on it and some red grips and a blue seat.

I used to get it out at the weekend we used to go on the field there used to be me peter and Ian. My bike was the best then peters then Ian. Ian was not a good rider and his bike was the slowist. When I used to get on it and kik it up it was a very good felling and it always used to be at the frunt then peter and then Ian allways last

When we used to get home we used to help eache uther clean aware bikes.

Technical difficulties do not appear to have prevented the flow of Gregory's narrative because now he is writing from his own personal centre of experience. The piece echoes the same confidence he shows when leading his team of riders: 'it always used to be at the frunt then peter and then Ian allways last'. He describes the thrill he feels starting up his bike: 'when I used to get on it and kik it up was a very good felling'.

Gregory recalls his accident narrating the episode in detail and he is not afraid to reveal his fear when he sees the cut on his knee and writes 'sundley I started to panic I did'tn now what to do'. He also attempts to convey the speed at which he was receiving medical treatment for he adds 'like a flash I was laying on the opurating table to be sticked up'.

After this event, Gregory had 'to get rid of the bike' which caused him much sadness. Referring back to the taped discourse. Gregory had appeared to identify with the 'maleness' of the bike in his reference to the bike being 'him': 'he can't do it he teks 'im to the garage'. It would not be my intention here to interpret Gregory's work in the psychoanalytic way that say Holbrook (1964) did. However, it is unavoidable to comment that this identity occurred at a time when Gregory was undergoing medical examinations to find out why his overall physical growth and that of his genitals was not progressing at the rate one would expect for an adolescent boy of nearly fifteen. So, in one sense, for Gregory the loss of his bike could be equated with his own loss of maleness. His next written piece shows Gregory's attempts to resolve this by transferring his sense of loss onto a mother figure, which is again interesting as Gregory's parents were separated and he was brought up by his father:

Motorbike
Seeing you on the road
Your mother fears
the risk you take.
Petrol ... oil ... bits
And hours mending
The bike.
The money you've saved
For the part you want.
Now you're on the road
Looking out
All around.
The feel of power
In your hands
The grip getting more sweaty
With the movement
Of your hands.
But I got rid of the bike.

Here Gregory 'got rid of the bike' because his mother feared him riding it, not because in reality, he crashed the bike during his accident. By transferring the loss in this way, Gregory does not lose his own sense of personal dignity; losing the bike was simply not his fault.

Through the medium of writing, children with special needs like Gregory can try to come to terms with, and to communicate, inner fears and feelings of anxiety. It may have been sufficient for the teacher to regard his efforts both on tape and through writing as being no more than work about bikes: being aware of the pupil as a person meant that the teacher could understand more fully the value of his attempts.

With Gregory, the starting point for communicating through writing had been the loss of his bike, for Chris, the loss of his mother during his fifth year at school, was the cause of a very detailed account of his mourning:

A Funeral
As I walked out of the house, I felt the ice cold wind on my face. Gillian was already in the car when I got outside. The funeral car came from J. Lunts, which is on Abbeydale Road, and they were very polite. People stared at me as if there was something wrong with me. The engine of the car was as quiet as a mouse, and the car went very slowly.

When we arrived outside the church, I noticed that we pulled up behind the hearse in which my mother lay. I looked at my father, and he was looking at the coffin, and he must have been thinking about her, because water appeared in his eyes. I was very tense by now, because my hands were wet with perspiration, and I was breathing deeply through my mouth.

There was one thing I thought of, when I looked at the coffin. It was the pictures which we have taken, when we all went on holiday to Italy. The ones which contained my mother, seemed false somehow. The doors of the car were opened at two minutes to nine. When we were all out of the car, the coffin was lifted out as if it contained gold; it was handled with great care. There were four men carrying the coffin one was on each corner.

She was slowly carried up the steps to the church, in front of her family. My mother's father, waited at the top of the steps in a dark doorway until the coffin had passed him: then he walked in with us. The coffin was placed onto a frame which had four wheels on it and it was pushed slowly until it reached the bottom of the steps, leading up to the altar. I felt everyone look at me as I walked down the church so I observed the detail on one part of the coffin and thought of the memories I had of her.

The priest came down and shook hands with the members of her family. As one of the readings was read I kept thinking of what the doctor had said. He said that she was a strong, loving and courageous women because she didn't tell my sisters or myself that she was not going to live much longer. I remember making her drinks and something to eat; and talking to her about how I was going to help her to walk again.

I stopped day dreaming when I heard the priest talking about my mother. He asked God to give us strength to overcome this difficult period. At that point I heard my Auntie Gloria crying. My grandad was sitting on the left side of me and I saw him turning the pages of a hymn book like a child does when he doesn't understand what is going on. Alison was using her hanky, Gillian who is the oldest in the three children was in tears with Alison crying I felt so alone. Tears appeared in my eyes but I was determined not to cry because my mother would cry if she saw me cry for her. Two songs were sung during the mass and it was so good that it sounded like a choir of angels singing from heaven.

When the mass came to an end the coffin was taken and carried out of the church by four men from Lunts. As we followed her out of the church I noticed the church was full. We entered the hired car again when the coffin was placed in the hearse. All the people that knew us came over to us to say how sorry they were. There was one woman from the Civil Service, which was the place where my mother worked whose name was Karen. They were best colleagues at work. Karen was crying continuously as she looked at my mother's coffin. Her eyes were red from crying and she couldn't believe that she had died; she shook her head in disbelief. Her workmates were going to send lots of different types of flowers so that she could be cheered up by them, but this didn't happen.

My grandad entered the car with us and he was still in another world because he wasn't upset. The funeral cortege left for the cemetery which was on Abbey Lane. The clouds looked down on us in anger and the wind was as fierce as a lion that was wild. The priest said a few words and she was then lowered into the ground. I thought to myself. 'Where do I look? to God, below to the ground or up to the sky?'

I wanted to go home so I stood next to the car with my dad. The flowers at the edge of her grave didn't look to be much but they were from people's own money to show how much everyone loved her. It looked like a mountain of flowers.

When we arrived at our home it seemed empty mentally because she didn't exist and I felt a part of me disappear. I took my suit off when I entered the house and made drinks for anyone that wanted one because she told me once to help when she was gone. I only wished I knew because then I would have stayed in and not had any argument with anyone.

The guests which came back to the house asked to help but my father didn't want any help because he knew that we could cope by ourselves as a family. My father talked about her illness to his friends and showed them photographs of her last holiday which was in Italy at a resort called Rimini. She really enjoyed herself that year because she went three times with Gillian. When I found out that she had bought me a Christmas present I just went upstairs and it all poured out. My tears came like the water running from a tap. The day seemed to be never-ending but there is one person that I will never forget and that is my mother.

(Chris: aged 16)

Until he had written this, Chris had caused the teachers much concern as he became withdrawn and showed reluctance to talk through his grief.

Through his writing, Chris is emphasising the creative nature of communication. By making his feelings public he is showing that he exists as a personality with an identity and a self-image in a social world. The proposition 'I communicate therefore I am' argues that communication is an act of conferment, of creation of identity and of reality. It is through writing that one is able to reflect. By putting feelings on to paper, we are enabled to define and re-define our emotions as Chris did when he wrote about his mother's death. The same depth of feeling came from Matthew, a fourth-year pupil from a mixed ability group, who wrote of the death of a kitten:

The Death of a Kitten

One afternoon, my kitten fell asleep in
The washing-machine curled up in
A blanket. While he was there, my
Mother was looking for him. She
Shut the door of the washing-machine
And started to wash the blanket.
She carried on looking for it.
She came in to hang
The blanket out and he fell out
With its neck broken. It was dead.

(Matthew: aged 14)

This is more than a simple re-telling of an experience. The reference to the kitten as 'he' then later as 'it', demonstrates that Matthew distances the experience. His coming to terms with it, is represented by a linguistic shift as the live kitten becomes a dead thing. Matthew, through his writing, unlocks the memory of a painful experience which he is then able to share and make public.

That personal writing is a medium through which especially withdrawn adolescents come to terms with their problems has been the subject of a book by Bernard Harrison (1986) entitled *Sarah's Letters: A Case of Shyness*. In this, an extremely shy pupil wrote a series of letters to her English teacher which communicated a deepening dissidence from her school attachments. They focus on her growing sense of isolation and detachment caused by her shyness and lack of self-assertion. Harrison's sensitive account of Sarah's struggle towards gaining more self-confidence alerts teachers to the problems of shyness and demonstrates how some enhanced form of teacher–learner relationships is needed to help pupils to gain confidence in themselves. Similar approaches to writing either in the form of letters, journals or autobiographies can be a valuable means of encouraging some individuals with special needs to communicate their problems to a trusted confidant. Such was the case of Katrina who, unlike Sarah, was labelled by her teachers as 'Trouble with a capital T'. Her reputation for being disruptive had preceded her together with a medley of psychologist reports, lists of day to day incidents, copies of letters home to parents and so forth. In all, she was openly violent and aggressive towards the authority structure of her school. Katrina was reluctant to speak and her reticence conveyed a smouldering contempt interpreted as 'dumb insolence' by her teachers. She was a very able fourth-year pupil who was put in the 'remedial group' because of her behavioural problems and disaffection with school.

In addition to writing her autobiography and pieces for formal course work assessment, Katrina wrote many letters to her English teacher who was also in charge of her welfare as pastoral care tutor. The letters were usually written at crisis points during her schooling when she felt that she couldn't talk to her teacher about her problems and in one letter admits 'the only time I talk is if it's for a good reason'. While the scope of this book does not allow extensive inclusion of every letter, the following example illustrates how this form of writing was allowing Katrina to communicate her feelings. Previous to writing it, Katrina had played truant and was later excluded from school for swearing at her form teacher.

28th February

Dear Miss Walsh,
    Over the holiday I have been thinking about the apologies I have to make and I think I owe one to you for running away like I did. I should

have thought before doing it. I suppose I should also say I'm sorry to my form teacher and to the headmaster for causing all the trouble I did but I daren't. Also I should say I'm sorry for smashing all the ornaments on the bar in our house when you brought me home. I just got mad and I didn't know what else to do.

I'm going to try to be good by not cheeking teachers and keeping quiet in lessons. Tomorrow, I've got housecraft. I was always messing about in that lesson and maths today, Wednesday and Friday, I never like that. Every time I play truant it's always on a maths day; I've missed loads of them lessons. But I'll change all that now and go to every lesson and work and even do the homework and bring it in on time. I know I still won't probably like school, but at least I'll leave with SOME good thoughts, I might even miss some people.

To me, school is a place you have to come to, and when you're there it doesn't matter what you do. I know I can't do that now, I've got to behave. It's like the P. E. teacher said earlier, I don't stand a chance of getting a job if I get expelled; my reports are all too bad and it's too late to try and change them now but I can at least add a few good points to them.

Well, maybe I'll get up enough courage to see my form teacher after registration and apologise to him. The only trouble is, different people are saying different things and I can't change over night and some people think I can well it's impossible.

That's all I can write so I'll just say I'm sorry for everything and I'll try and change but I won't promise anything.

Love from
Katrina

Katrina and the teacher still keep up a steady correspondence, no different from any exchange of news between friends.

Many pupils like Katrina show disaffection with school while others show their avoidance of a living engagement with the world through underground patterns of behaviour. Such was the case with Sara, a fifth-year pupil from a mixed-ability group, who fell prey to the habit of glue sniffing. The first time that the school became aware of her problem was when she was caught by the police for stealing glue from a local shop. It had been difficult for her to come back to school, so on her return, her teacher had a quiet, re-assuring chat to Sara. The following is how she described her feelings when under the influence of glue:

Teacher: Do you feel better when you take glue?
Sara: You feel happy like.
Teacher: You feel.
Sara: You feel — it fills you up.
Teacher: With what? With sort of different emotions you mean?
Sara: Yeh.

After talking rather reluctantly at this stage about her experiences, Sara volunteers to write about what she's been through:

Sara: You know like in this thing? wi t'different emotions and that.
Teacher: Mm.
Sara: Well — I could write something on that.
Teacher: That'd be lovely! Yes, yeh, either in the form of a poem, story or a letter to me. Alright?
Sara: Yeh, alright.

The piece that Sara produced was a detailed account of her experiences entitled 'Glue-sniffing: Your Feelings' of which the following is an extract:

> When you are under the influence of glue, your feelings can differ, all depending on your surroundings. If the people around you are in a happy mood, you too become in a happy mood. If you're on your own while sniffing, you become lonely. It contains many different emotions, so you cannot really say that it makes you either one or the other.
>
> When you first start sniffing you can get very confused. When I first started I didn't know what was happening to me. When you have your first few breathes you become very dizzy. Then you have to sit down to get used to the feeling. Then as you get higher a buzzing sound comes to your head and if no one tells you what is happening you may start shouting or screaming.
>
> Not all people do this, some may just sit quiet while they are sniffing. As you breath more and more glue, it starts to go dark and you get a kind of fuzzy eye sight. It's as if it were snowing. This is when you are beginning to get really high. Then if you continue, your mind goes and you don't know what you are doing and you have no will-power to control what you are doing because you don't know your're doing it. Well you do at the time but it's as if it wasn't real. I forgot to mention after you have your first few breathes your voice changes. It sounds as if you were a very slow person. Your legs also begin to go and you start to walk funny.
>
> If you have enough glue, when you come down after so long, you can't remember sometimes what you have done within the few hours that you were high.

The writing continues extensively, much in the same style, unfolding in detail the hallucinatory dreams that glue sniffing effects:

> … As we were about to go all the rest of the lads came down and Miffer had a big tin that they had put together to buy. So we decided to have some but said that we weren't stopping for long and we also said that we

were only having a few breathes. In the end we stopped for about three hours because once you start you don't want to stop. You can guess how much we had because I started with the dreams again and so did the others.

I was only having short dreams and in one dream I dreamt that my bag was melting and I chucked the bag and all the glue went all over the windows of the school, so we had to go because the caretaker was chasing us. When we went back onto the school premises, big tall lad called Maris was having a dream and in his dream he saw a white dove going through a hole in the window and as this dove flew in, the hole got smaller so that the dove couldn't get back out. To get the dove out Maris smashed the window where the hole was to make it bigger to get the bird out and as the window smashed he came round. When he realized what he had done we all started running and it took some time to lose the caretaker but we finally managed to lose him.

At the end of the account which took place over several weeks, Sara no longer felt the need to take glue. Through talking and then through writing, Sara had re-lived the experiences and had eventually come to terms with herself and reached a point of self-realisation.

SUMMARY

A proposition 'I communicate therefore I am' emphasises the creative nature of communication. It means that one exists as a personality with an identity and self image in the social world. This chapter has demonstrated how writing can help pupils with special needs to communicate their true feelings and to come to terms with their true self. Once the learner has been encouraged to write from his or her own personal centre of experience, it is easier for them to improve upon their more obvious difficulties such as spellings, syntax, punctuation and handwriting. The importance of talk as a prerequisite to writing has also been stressed.

Communication Through the Expressive Arts

All pupils need access to the arts, including drama, music and the visual arts.

(ILEA, 1984, 3, 4, 20, p. 40)

An expressive arts approach to learning allows English Studies to entwine with disciplines such as dance, drama, music and film. One authority had this to say:

It follows, that as teachers of language we should recognise the primary importance for our lives of all the expressive arts — kinetic, visual, musical, literary, verbal. As learners or teachers, we seek then to be continually engaged and re-engaged in arts disciplines — especially, of course, in the language arts of literature, drama, art-speech. These are the disciplines through which English studies will flourish, and which offer, at best, a true basis for any genuinely individual expression of experience.

(Harrison, 1983a, p. 7)

What is being shown here, is how art is the revealed experience of our own living, our own being. We express and communicate our visions of experience through making the forms of art. This view echoes that of D. H. Lawrence who, through his character Ursula, in *Women in Love* (Lawrence, 1921) declared that 'the word of art is only the truth about the real world, that's all.' Personal research suggests that an arts-based approach to teaching children with special needs can be an effective means of encouraging the communication and expression in which they seem to lack confidence.

Teachers of children with special needs still insist on giving their pupils a diet of 'the basics' in terms of reading and writing which totally ignores the pupils' emotional development. Such attitudes fail to acknowledge that the expressive arts develop in pupils, a unique way of knowing.

By adopting an arts-based approach it would often be necessary to allow the pupils to work through another medium before attempting to communicate through the more conventional aspects of their language curriculum. Working in this way adds another dimension to the process of symbol-making that the pupils are trying to elaborate and make explicit. In this way, we show that our language has a poetic basis and seeks embodiment in the many forms of expression — spoken, musical, written, painted — of arts discourse. To give a practical application of this process, Richard's work provides an example. Richard, a fourth-year pupil, in a mixed-ability group, had been labelled as having 'dyslexia', and also suffered intermittent hearing loss. The following extract from the teacher's journal describes how Richard first became involved with mushrooms:

25th January
Sylvia Plath's poem *Mushrooms* provided the class with a starting point for the pupils' spoken and written response. Richard showed some reluctance to talk at first. I therefore encouraged him to communicate his response through an alternative medium — clay. Richard started modelling a mushroom shape. The poem had provided him with an expressive impulse and he needed a different medium than talk or writing in order to resolve his response to it.

Later Richard complemented his model with some photographs he took of fungi growing in the park near school. The model and photographs acted as 'holding forms' to centre the impulse before Richard proceeded toward refinement; he also came to a better understanding of Plath's realized form:

Teacher: (re-reads poem) Now what's your impression after you've listened to that poem?

Richard: er — I think it's a good poem.

Teacher: Mm.

Richard: er — and I like the way it describes the — the people as they keep trying to grow and they're taking over the world.

Teacher: Oh yes — Mm

Richard: 'So many of us ... '

Teacher: So you think the mushrooms are what we call 'personified' — made to seem like people?

Richard: Yeh.

Richard now feels confident to take tentative steps to disclose how he thinks Plath's is 'a good poem'. Without any prompting from the teacher who initially provides a sort of 'floating attention' in the discourse, Richard goes on to explain that the mushrooms to him 'seem to be people'. At this point, the teacher considers that Richard is ready to be introduced to the term 'personification' and affirms his understanding of the concept during the subsequent dialogue:

Teacher: Good — OK, And is there any little bit that you like especially? Any lines — or ...
Richard: (pause) The last — er — two verses.
Teacher: Mm.
Richard: 'Nudgers' ... from 'nudgers' to erm — 'our foot's in the door'.
Teacher: Yeh and why do you like that bit?
Richard: Just do.
Teacher: What picture do you get in your mind with those two versus then that you ... makes you like them so much?
Richard: Keep thinking of the globe and ... (Richard here uses a broad gesture to suggest 'roundness'.)
Teacher: Oh yes — oh.
Richard: All these mushrooms start taking over.

Both teacher and pupil feel relaxed enough to allow time for answers to be formulated; they no longer fear hesitations and pauses but respect the need for silences. Richard initially finds it difficult to explain why he likes the last two stanzas of Plath's poem. His terse reply, 'Just do', prompts the teacher to guide Richard to help him clarify what he is struggling to say, so she asks: 'What picture do you get in your mind?'. His reply, 'Keep thinking of the globe and ... ', qualifies that thinking in images is thinking in feeling. But in addition to this, Richard's use of gesture to suggest 'roundness' indicates that in order to represent his subjective response, he uses every means available to him to convey meaning. The teacher helps him come to terms with his personal response by questioning him about his model of mushrooms:

Teacher: And when you started doing your own model of the mushrooms, how did you start with that? Did you just get the base first and then go from ...
Richard: Cut the base out yes and then stuck a stem.
Teacher: ... Mm.
Richard: ... and t'top was the hardest bit. I worked it flat an' then I thought: no mushroom's flat and so it's got to be curved.
Teacher: Mm.
Richard: So that were a bit hard so then I lap — started to overlap it.

Richard's struggle to 'get it right' is no less than that experienced by other artists. He openly admits how 'top was the hardest bit' of the mushroom to make and it also demonstrates how Richard closely observed its form: 'an' then I thought: no mushroom's flat and so it's got to be curved' and again Richard found 'that were a bit hard'. He remembers what real mushrooms look like and through his senses, translates his previous knowledge into a new, personal awareness. As he explains how he overcame the problem, his talk becomes more explicit: 'I lap — started to overlap it'. This same struggle will be repeated later as Richard conveys meaning through writing. The teacher next emphasised to Richard that his symbol is valid and worthy of discussion.

Teacher: Mm … Mm and some of the words in this poem really you've tried to sum up, I think, in your model and in your own poem as well. You've got — erm — where it says they're pushing through — don't you? And you've got — erm — the 'small grains make room' 'soft fists' — what picture does that give you? 'soft fists insist'.

Richard: Like er — like — er — a little arm pushing up out of the ground.

Teacher: Do you think that's a good summary of how mushrooms grow?

Richard: Yeh.

Teacher: Mm and you thought they might be people as well.

The teacher affirms for Richard that his mushroom model has so far captured the essence of the expressive impulse and stands side by side with Sylvia Plath's poem. Again, Richard is finding it difficult to clarify his response to the image created by the phrase 'soft fists insist': the teacher simply asks 'what picture does that give you?' and Richard creates his own simile: 'Like — er — a little arm pushing up out of the ground.' Because Richard is displaying a more confident response to the poem, the teacher next risks guiding him into realising how the form of a poem can help convey meaning:

Teacher: What do you notice about the way that it's set out? Is there anything that strikes you then?

Richard: Yeh it's all neat t' it's all roughly three lines.

Teacher: Mm and what — does that give any particular effect?

Richard: Yeh — short — er — each verse is short — er — each verse is short and quickly gone.

Teacher: Yes there are lots of verses aren't there?

Richard: Yeh and with it being lots of verses it makes it sound as if it's growing as it goes along.

Teacher: Good. Yes that's a good point.

There is no need for the teacher to complicate the discourse by introducing poetical terms because, unlike earlier when she realised

Richard was ready to accept 'personification', here he is still thinking through the meaning as he talks. Instead, the teacher purposely makes her replies simple: 'Yes there are lots of verses aren't there?' as she patiently waits for Richard to organise his response when he then admits 'and with it being lots of verses it makes it sound as if it's growing as it goes along'. Now the teacher feels Richard is ready to explore the text further:

Teacher: What do you notice about the — the — erm — the sound of some of the words. Is there anything that strikes you about the sounds?

Richard: Er — (pause) On each verse they — most of 'em seem to rhyme.

Teacher: Mm. I thought — em — 'very discreetly, quietly' 'nosing the loam', what else, 'fists insist' — that's interesting.

Richard: It's like on a conveyor — like a little conveyor belt spinning it round. (uses gesture to show 'spinning') (Both laugh at this remark.)

Teacher: Alright. Now is there anything else you want to say about it?

Richard: Mm — that bit er 'no voice ... voiceless' and 'no eyes, the ears' — its so — simple form.

Teacher: Mm. Right very interesting — good — well done. Thanks very much Richard.

After Richard has mentioned that the stanzas rhyme, the teacher indulges in phrases which have an onomatopoeic quality and she enjoys repeating them aloud for Richard to appreciate the full effect of Plath's language. This prompts Richard to form another personal simile 'It's like on a conveyor — like a little conveyor belt'. Again he qualifies his meaning through gesture, and the rapport between teacher and pupil is so anxiety-free that they both laugh at this explanation. The teacher invites Richard to add further comment and he similarly adopts the teacher's earlier indulgence of language as he repeats lines which have a particular appeal: 'no voice ... voiceless' and 'no eyes, the ears', until finally he comes to realise fully that the meaning is conveyed by the form: 'its so — simple form'.

This appreciation of Plath's realised form gives Richard the confidence to make a similar attempt after he had used his mushroom model to hold his creative impulse. Before the final draft emerged, he used the word processor so that he could edit his own work:

> In the damp night we grow
> Slowly growing upwards to the sky
> Our grey tops like hammers we push up

> People don't notice
> us pushing to take over the world.
> Tables or hammers
> We move up slowly, slowly
> Moving the soil to make room
> for more of us.
> Our roots dangle in the rotting
> vegetables, mouldy logs and in the
> damp grass.
> But we can only grow so far
> When some people go and eat us
> They think we look nice to eat
> But some of us are not so tasty
> Than those murderous cannibals
> So get ill or die,
> Some of us live on to grow.

While Richard has followed the style of Plath closely, his writing is undoubtedly a personal celebration of growth. He maintains the central image throughout in phrases such as 'we grow', 'slowly growing upwards' 'only grow' 'live on to grow' and 'our roots dangle' which are the more obvious examples. Earlier in the spoken dialogue, Richard was introduced to the concept of 'personification' and here he uses the technique with confidence. But more importantly, Richard identifies with the mushrooms so that their growth becomes a symbol for his own.

Richard previously needed to use gesture to convey the sense of roundness, now it gives way to a confident, controlled use of assonance to create the same effect through the sustained 'oh' sound of 'grow/slowly growing', 'mouldy' and 'take over the world', so effecting the roundness of the mushrooms.

Richard's working through a variety of media in order to form an understanding, demonstrates how we each express and communicate our vision of experience through making various forms of art. The more Richard became involved in this process, the more he gained confidence in language. This illustrates how the true quest of language is that of living from the body's experience. Again, we can turn to Harrison for comment:

> For our very being is lodged in our language, as our language it is our being: and only through our language can we declare ourselves to others to the world, thus validating both ourselves and the world.
> (Harrison, 1983a, p. 9)

Discovering the world through touch, vision, hearing, smelling, tasting and giving shapes to these discoveries in language forms: these are bodily acts through which personal meanings are offered and shared. Of the expressive arts drama is an accessible means through which children with special needs can share this living engagement. The next illustration shows how the teacher used the theme of 'diaries' as a means of encouraging expressive exploration of texts. After improvising scenes from favourites such as *The Diary of Anne Frank* (Frank, 1947) and Sue Townsend's *The Secret Diary of Adrian Mole* (Townsend, 1982), this fourth-year lower-band group were introduced to Edith Holden's *The Diary of An Edwardian Lady* (Holden, 1906) in an attempt to extend the pupils' awareness of wider issues concerning preservation and conservation.

The teacher began by showing the pupils a real nest which she had purposely hidden from view at first so that there would be some element of surprise to the opening of the lesson. The first indication of an active engagement to this came from Elizabeth who shrieked when she saw the nest and excitedly exclaimed 'we've got one like this in our garden'. Such spontaneous 'now' moments are when the pupils are showing a willingness to form a 'connecting' in the learning event. These moments rely next on the teacher's skill to sustain her pupils' quickened interest. She swiftly leads the group on to discuss the social issues of nesting. The group seem eager to relate personal anecdotes for example, Gerry said that he found some blackbird's eggs one day: this was followed by Caroline's tale:

Teacher: So Gerry — did you think it was right to take those eggs?
Caroline: No.
Gerry: I left them.
Caroline: Well my neighbour — isn't it quiet? — well my neighbour — erm — is called Mr Vickers. Well once he was complaining or something anyway. He — erm — came up and pinched our birds' nest and it had all t'chicks in and eggs and dat. He just knocked it down an' left it on our garden and we had to clear it up.

It is noticed how Caroline joins in Gerry's exchange with the teacher as if there is an attempt to communicate with each other. Caroline next becomes aware that the whole group is willing to listen actively to her anecdote by her remark 'isn't it quiet?' This incident which Caroline retells had evidently made a lasting impression. Her memory is jogged in a way that she feels she must share her experience with the group and her sensitivity towards her environment is later revealed during an improvisation documented below.

The teacher then read the poem '*Birds' Nests*' by Edward Thomas and asked the group to work in pairs. One pupil had to decide whether or not to steal eggs from a nest they had found. The pupils had to put forward reasons for not stealing eggs and to persuade their friend to do likewise. One of the most revealing reactions came from the conversation between Mark and Caroline. After Mark had threatened Caroline not to touch the imagined eggs, he tried the art of gentle persuasion by appealing to her better judgement:

Caroline: I know, well, they would be mine if I tek 'em.
Mark: Yes, but dey're not yours now doh are dey?
Caroline: No, that's why I'm going to tek 'em.
Mark: Listen, dis likkle bird hasn't worked all winter to keep dese eggs warm just for you to tek 'em (long pause) ... Nah I've left ye speechless (Caroline giggles) don't know what to say! You should be ashamed of ye sen.

The couple were evidently enjoying this argument and after finding further debate, Mark quite unexpectedly manipulated the improvision by spontaneously announcing.

Mark: Anyway, I'm going to that pond ...
Caroline: Pond?
Mark: Yeh.
Caroline: What pond?
Mark: Dat fish pond down deer wi' all t'fishes in, I'm going to get t'fish (laughs as if he is aware of his provocative remark).
Caroline: I thought 'what's up wi' you? If you don't want me to get these birds' eggs and then you're going to nick the fish! I'll report you to the RSPCA.'
Mark: Ah well dat's diff'rnt doh in it?
Caroline: No, it's exactly the same thing.

The whole discussion had thus reversed its implications. Mark later told Caroline that he needed fish for 'his dinner', which suggested the idea of needing fish for one's own basic survival. Thus by the end of this conversation, a fuller deeper understanding had been reached between these two pupils.

   The pupils formed a larger group to develop the next sequence of improvisation. The teacher asked them to imagine that they had gone for a walk on the moors when they met two men who showed them some live vipers which had been found. As the men handled the creatures, the group were asked to discuss the fate of these — should they be killed or not? The improvisation developed to the time the party returned to the country cottage and during the evening as they relaxed after their walk, the gamekeeper's wife from a neighbouring cottage showed the group two stuffed specimens of a night-jar. These birds are very rare — could it be because the nests are frequently robbed? This suggestion provided an opportunity for the earlier dialogue, concerning reasons for and against leaving nests untouched, to be re-introduced at this point. The teacher then role-played one of the party who decided to write up notes in her journal about the day's events. In role, the teacher read extracts from Edith Holden's diary (the entry for April 23rd–28th) to summarise how the sequence of events had been recorded. The teacher could easily have begun with the diary entry and simply asked the group to 'act it out' but by leaving the extract until last, the actual text formed the climax of the lesson and thus assumed more importance. It was also seen to be more 'in context' within the group's own improvisation. Still in role, the teacher invited added comments for inclusion in her diary. The session culminated in the teacher showing the group a copy of *The Diary of an Edwardian Lady* which the pupils regarded as artistically beautiful from their many comments. As Edith Holden's delicate watercolours made strong appeal, a follow-up lesson included encouraging the group to attempt sketches for a similar countryside notebook. In this case, the literature had not been used as a starting point and then discarded, rather the role-play and improvisations had led the group towards a clearer understanding of the text.

LANGUAGE GROWTH THROUGH PUPPETRY

In any given group, there are bound to be some pupils with special needs who do not willingly communicate through the expressive arts in the way previously outlined. Such pupils are likely to be at some disadvantage in their attempts to establish learning and social relationships. Equally, when there are snarls and tangles in a pupil's emotional growth, they become manifest in language difficulties which thus reduce the capacity to communicate in order to form relationships. One approach towards helping timid and withdrawn individuals to realise their inherent creative capacity, is that of puppetry. The puppets act as a catalyst, as a medium for expression and for the forming of relationships.

The value of puppetry within the field of therapy has long been known. Yet there is a natural reserve for puppets to be employed in secondary schools with pupils who find difficulty in communicating. This led to some small-scale research during which the teacher worked with a small group of first-year pupils in a mixed comprehensive school who were regarded by their subject teachers to be timid, and who might benefit from working in a small group within a non-competitive climate. What follows is an account of the research which demonstrates how the pupils at first found it difficult to reveal their true selves, because circumstances had not, until then, permitted their selves to emerge. But when given time, space and freedom — a medium for change and growth — they gained the confidence and trust to grow beyond rigidity and timidity. The puppets acted as 'holding forms' during this period of confusion while the true self emerged and language developed.

After the first meeting with the pupils it was felt that, despite their aptitude for adequate spoken language, they previously felt no desire to communicate, either because they had not been sufficiently motivated, or because they had not been given the appropriate opportunities to realise their verbal skills in practice — even more fundamentally, perhaps, no one would listen to them.

From the outset it was noticed that the pupils' language was 'limited' in so far as their vocabulary was not extensive and they found it difficult to sustain a conversation. There were occasions, though, when their dialogue was full of vitality, description and wit — especially from Michael. At this stage, the prime concern was seen to be that of creating the contexts and conditions in which further language could develop by encouraging talk in a friendly, non-competitive climate. By developing discourse creatively, perhaps sentence structure would improve; a refining of vocabulary would only come through an increased sensitivity to words.

By encouraging, not demanding, hopefully the atmosphere would become one of mutual trust through which the pupils could develop their language and from which the often neglected component of oracy, that of listening, could be promoted. This necessitated placing the refinement of language secondary to the overall aim of promoting conversation and yet still maintain this initial vigour and vitality of expression.

During the second session the group were involved in making a sculptured face from plasticine on which to apply papier mâché. Parts of the procedure were being recorded on video of which Peter appeared very conscious:

Peter: (aware of video) Miss, is it going to watch us? Miss I've rolled mine funny! I might look like a spastic.
Julian: Yeah, you are, aren't you?
Teacher: Then, when you've got it into a ball ...
Peter: (towards the camera) Smile!
Teacher: ... put it on top of the toilet roll and start moulding it into a face.
Peter: I bet she starts filming while I'm goin to do dis (rolling).

These exchanges were not meant as hurtful taunts, as for example the samples of competition and conflict, but were rather playful insults, which were repeated similarly later in the proceedings when each other's models were criticised. As part of the time was involved with filming or with helping individuals with their models, there were periods when the teacher did not actually address them and the pupils could not vie for attention as much as previously, so they were able to talk to each other in a more exploratory capacity:

Peter: I'm making a silly Wards for Wardy — nick, nicks, nick, nack.
(pause — Michael humming and singing to himself)
How much do you get a day for school?
Andrew: Two or three pounds.
Peter: Oh I bet! bet tha' nicked it! How many bruvvers has tha got Gibney?
Andrew: What?
Peter: How many bruvvers has tha got?
Andrew: None, none.
Peter: How many sisters?
Andrew: Five.
Michael: Ah, you don't you do it on top o' theer (helping Andrew).

This illustrates how the individuals are beginning to become curious about each other and seek additional background information by questionings. Intimacy is gained by referring to surnames, 'Wardy' for Ward and 'Gibney', and by the moves Michael makes to help Andrew.

Peter increasingly demonstrated his anxiety about the video, even to the extent that he monitored his feelings aloud and would suddenly begin talking about the video, assuming his listeners knew to what he was referring. This could be termed as 'language of implicit meaning' in that the individual qualification of meaning is implicit in the speaker's sentence organisation:

Peter: Miss, look! I've done a neck... will it be going to protestant schools an' all, will it come on for school?
(pause of 25 seconds, during which time they roll plasticine)
(Aloud) Act as if you don't know it's deer when she does it.

And similarly later he asked whether 'it was working':

Peter: Miss, is it working now?
Teacher: Nearly.
Peter: What do you mean 'nearly'?

Teacher: Well the camera's not started.
Peter: Will you let me know when it's started?

The camera is also personified as someone watching. 'Miss t'camera keeps looking at Gibney an' him. Take One!'
  Evident from this is the anxiety they have that the task in hand must meet with approval. They needed constant reassurance that they were fulfilling the correct procedure as when Julian asks 'shall I put the head back?' or Andrew's remark 'Can I make a moustache?' or Peter's 'can I make a ghost?' and Michael's 'How big can you make the nose Miss? As big as you want?' It was very marked that Elaine was the only one of the group who could work independently towards completing the task, without even requiring to explore the first stage of tactile experience which the boys found necessary in their first manipulations of the plasticine. Their preliminary investigations were playful and experimental in which they moulded the material to various concrete imitations, 'look at my bent banana,' 'mine looks like a fried egg' and with a piece of brown plasticine there was the remark, 'it's bob-baa, I'm going to chuck this down t'bog'. This same playfulness permeated in their first attempts at creating a head and face:

Peter: Hey, mine looks like one of t'muskateers dun't it?
Michael: No, it looks like someone with bags under their eyes.
Julian: That's his moustache.

Even so, they were genuinely interested in each other's efforts and tentatively remarked about the models:

Michael: Have you seen the uvver side of Julian's Miss? (giggles)
Peter: Let's have a look Julian.
Michael: He's doing Worzel Gummidge.
Peter: Look at Wardy's (laughs) (then to Elaine) That's good!

Not only were there thus the occasional attempts to communicate with each other, but they were attempting to lead the teacher into the conversation, perhaps for re-assurance, they also recognised the worth of Elaine's effort.
  There has been substantive evidence, mainly from Barnes and Todd (1977), to suggest that under certain circumstances, pupils are able to talk to good purpose and to increase their understanding without calling on adult resources, as the teacher's role as director of the interaction is no longer applicable. While this was not particularly the case during the session observed, it was noticed that when the teacher remained unobtrusive, the boys would show a

capacity to sustain a desultory conversation. One such example revolved around the topic of football:

Peter: Miss, Liverpool are playing tomorrow against Man. United for t'cup.
Michael: Oh Sheffield Wednesday are playing tonight they're going to murder 'em.
Peter: Liverpool 'll win Man. United.
Michael: We'll kill yore.
Andrew: Everton's crowned ...
Peter: They're not, they're playing at Wembley.
Michael: Sheffield Wednesday can beat 'em.
Peter: He's thick 'im he says that we're playing at Wednesday tomorrow.

While there is the lack of ability to sustain a reasoned argument, the exchange has been a salutary one in which they were at least made aware of different allegiances. Peter makes the initiating move and acts as 'gatekeeper' in an attempt to draw in a wider audience; as the teacher did not reply, Michael challenged by a strategy of 'one-upmanship' in which the passion for the team which he supports is acknowledged. Peter challenges again by adding that Liverpool are not playing at Wednesday — that is Wednesday's football ground. Characteristic of this is the strong identification the boys have with their team such as in 'we'll kill yore' and 'he says we're playing at Wednesday.' This began impersonally 'they're going to murder 'em' but as the security of the position was challenged more subjectivity was communicated by a more personal attitude for the teams. It was also noticed how Andrew, on the brink of a potentially explicit and figurative statement beginning 'Everton's crowned' became swamped by the enthusiasm of the other two.

Throughout the session were occasions when the half-formed puppets became instrumental to speech for example when Peter held a conversation with his puppet:

Peter: Oh his moustache is wrong ... look at his nose ... oh ... eek uh aah ... he's killed me (simulates a fight with puppet head).

This is seen to run parallel with identifications with other personalities and characters such as Julian's request 'Can I be Worzel Gummidge,' or 'Gatty Goon here,' 'Syd Snot 'ere,' and 'I'm Kenny Everett,' as if they are unable to come to terms with themselves but feel secure behind a facade of tag-names.

From the remarks given by individuals, the impression gained was that much of the children's stimulation came from television. This became evident during the third session. During this meeting, the group were involved with making papier mâché layers for the top of the plasticine base. As they were mixing the paste, the immediate reaction when experiencing the sensation was 'ugh' later to be expanded to, 'it's just like rice-pudding this.' The teacher asked the group to tell her which characters they had decided to make. Michael replied he was 'making a footballer', only to be blatantly contradicted by Peter:

Michael: I'm making a footballer Miss.
Peter: You're not! (adamantly) You can be the housekeeper, you can be the housekeeper and I can be the robber.
Julian: Yeh, heh, and he can nick yeh.
Peter: Pinch er a lot of ...
Julian: Money.
Peter: Money.
Julian: He's er walking down t'street and then he dances out and says, 'aah! He's pinched the money.'

Peter challenged Michael because his character, the footballer, would not adjust into Peter's story, which was subsequently to form the basic plot for the puppet-play. Julian is seen to be in collaboration with the suggested plot and the excitement of his approval is conveyed through the telegraphic replies, often monosyllabic and certainly colloquial in expression as in 'pinch' and 'nick'. At the same time, phrases such as 'he dances out' and the earlier simile 'it's just like rice pudding this' indicates the potential for vigorous expression.

There was a digression away from this plot towards a recapitulation of current television programmes which had, as their central theme, that of robbery and violence, as the following sequence illustrates:

Teacher: What kind of house have they taken if from — or have they robbed a bank ... ?
Peter: A very posh house.
Teacher: Hmm.
Peter: Like *Raffles*.
Michael: Have you ever watched *Raffles*? Oh I don't (giggles).
Peter: Did you ever watch that?
Teacher: I did occasionally, yes.
Peter: It was good, it was clever of him.
Teacher: Who is?

Peter:	Raffles, he had some good ideas him.
Teacher:	What kind of good ideas?
Michael:	For nicking things?
Peter:	Oh aye, see that one about er, er ... whatyercall it ... that pinching of t'turtle?
Michael:	No.
Peter:	It were right good, I'm telling you. He er pinched that van didn't he?
Andrew:	Turtle, yeh, he got dressed up didn't he?
Peter:	See all that money in that van?
Michael:	(putting a finger in the paste) It's just like rice-pudding this.
Teacher:	What do you think makes a good story?
Peter:	Miss, I know the heading — the Punch and Julian Show.
Teacher:	Yes, but you've been telling me about *Raffles* what do you think makes a good story?
Michael:	Raffles and B ...
Julian:	Bunny they call him.
Peter:	Oh, *Raffles*! I don't mean that you goosepot! I mean last night — did you watch it last night?
Andrew:	Oh yeh, all t'money they had.
Julian:	I know.
Peter:	They pinched that van, didn't they Gibney? They didn't know all that money were in did they?
Andrew:	No ... till it came all over on t'radio ... 'stop that van, with all t'money in it.'
Peter:	Two people had robbed t'bank.
Michael:	Oh, I saw that.

The sheer length of the duration of this exchange serves to illustrate the capacity to sustain a conversation on a topic of mutual interest, where the subject matter involves relating first-hand experience. What the group are unable to do at this stage, is to deduce from this any generalisations as shown by the reply to the question, 'What makes a good story?' Peter's notion of a 'good story' becomes synonymous with 'heading' and the title of 'Raffles and Bunny'. The fact that the teacher had to ask twice without gaining any definite response from them, indicated that the question was too far removed from their experience at that moment. Another observation was that in such moments of intense involvement with the subject matter, the group would use the vernacular, 'posh', 'nicked', 'pinched' and 'it were right good'; similarly, when names could not be remembered, to cope with the gap, phrases such as 'whatyercall it' or 'thing' would suffice. The substance of the discourse was made up entirely of concrete particulars which required implicit subject knowledge in order to be communicated with meaning.

In mutually supportive discourse of this nature, one notices the frequent use of sympathetic circularity such as 'did they?' 'wouldn't he?' 'didn't he?' 'I mean' 'like' 'you know', which either operate as indicators of a break in the process of putting one's thoughts into words, a break which the listener is invited to fill in for himself from the shared stock of unformulated opinions, or they seem to appeal for confirmation of what follows, taking the form of a question tag. This had bearing on the interplay of relationships here. Michael originally stated that he did not watch *Raffles*, but as the boys become more involved with an interesting and almost insular topic, for Michael, he firstly questions Peter: 'for nicking things?' then contributed with a suitable title, 'Raffles and B ...' and finally remarked that he saw this particular television episode: 'Oh, I saw that'. This indicated an attempt on Michael's part, to be included in the group discourse. The extract shows a reversal of earlier situations in previous sessions, where the teacher took the initiative for most of the conversation topics. After an opening question: 'What kind of a house have they taken it from?' the teacher left the pupils to develop the conversation, and was drawn into the discourse by them. The teacher tried to keep her comments in line with the pupils' references, trying not to say anything that would indicate any desire that they should talk of things other than television programmes. Rather, the teacher tried to communicate understandingly and simply, recognition within their frame of reference, hence, the tentative questions: 'What kind of good ideas?', 'Who is?' and 'What makes a good story?' This ensured that while she was a willing listener, the teacher was not preventing the intimacy of the pupils' discourse by trying to change its direction. The teacher wanted the group to lead the way now; she would follow. The pupils would be given room to set the pace in the 'workshop' and for her part, hopefully, the teacher would recognise the pupils' efforts at two-way communication with some concrete reality basis of a shared experience. Thus, the importance of making puppets together, was the instrumental objective.

When the initiative is left to the individuals they will select the ground upon which they feel greatest security, as all people proceed with a caution that will protect the integrity of their personality. So, while the continual references to television could be equated with a paucity of imagination, for these pupils they were safe concepts.

The fascination shown for 'robbery' was subsequently elaborated when Julian collaborates with Peter's earlier suggestion and says 'He's er walking down t'street and then he dances out and says "aah. He's pinched the money!'" The same theme becomes circulated throughout the session, taking on diverse forms and references, some of which are implied rather than being consciously made as the following mention of *Dick Turpin* suggests. The teacher enquired who the characters were, to which they replied:

Julian:	Er Spike and …
Peter:	PC Copper mine is.
Teacher:	PC Copper?
Julian:	Er Tick Durpin.
Elaine:	No, it's not Tick Durpin, it's Dick Turpin.
Michael:	Tick Dirkin, Tick Gherkin.
Andrew:	Dick Gherkin.

The mention of the highwayman is a direct link with the theme of robbery, but also the sequence elucidates a capacity within the group to use language creatively.

A recognised stage of language acquisition is the remarkable way the child practises sounds on his or her own without any apparent motive except the delight in increasing a command of the language. Many utterances are made, often characterised by such features as rhythmic patterns, assonance or alliteration, during which time the child may correct his or her own pronunciation, drilling himself or herself into various sound distinctions, substituting various lexical items in a sentence pattern. With the above sequence, the group seem to be taking pleasure in 'playing' with the name 'Dick Turpin', much to the disdain of Elaine who does not want to apply the same rules to this game although, nevertheless, she participates in it. Her contribution is a tone of reprimand as though asserting her authority over the boys, 'it's not Tick Durpin, it's Dick Turpin'.

Being keenly aware of the superficiality which could result, the teacher attempted to elicit responses in which feelings were explored. In so doing she found that some very valuable insights occurred. One example is found after the group had been discussing their puppet characters:

Teacher:	You know if these people were walking down the street what kind of person would they need to be if they suddenly saw two robbers?
Peter:	Miss, they'd suddenly say, 'oh what's that?'
Teacher:	Do you think the policemen would feel afraid?
Julian:	No.
Peter:	Miss, yeah.
Teacher:	When might they feel afraid?
Peter:	When someone had murdered someone.

Andrew: When they'd got a gun wiv 'em.
Teacher: Do you ever get scared ...
Peter: Miss yeah ...
Teacher: ... of anything?
Michael: You get scared of Sister Catherine (the headmistress).

Though one could criticise the vagueness of this question, the response was one which resulted in an outpouring of suppositions. Peter seemed eager to admit his feelings and is shown in the way he interrupted the question, 'Do you ever get scared of anything?' The hint that he was scared of the headmistress, implies that Michael knew Peter's school background intimately and of his indictable behaviour, or it could be the basis of the group's difficulty in the normal school setting, the fear of authority or of unknown areas.

Believing that a pupil will gain his or her feelings of security from predictable, consistent and realistic limitations, the teacher made routine essential in the anticipation that a gradual increasing ability to assume responsibility for themselves would result in an independence. Throughout the sessions she wanted to reassure the group that this specific period on the timetable would be associated with 'puppet-workshop' in a similar spirit to Axline (1964) and her consultations with Dibs. In this she commented that:

> I had hoped to help Dibs differentiate betwen his feelings and his actions. He seemed to achieve a bit of this. I also hoped to communicate to him the fact that this one hour was only a part of his existence, that it could not and should not take precedence over all other relationships and experiences, that all the time between the weekly sessions was important too. The value of any successful therapeutic experience, in my opinion, depends upon the balance that is maintained between what the individual brings into the sessions and what he takes out. If the therapy becomes the predominant and controlling influence in the individual's daily life then I would have serious doubts as to its effectiveness. I wanted Dibs to feel that he had responsibility to take away with him his increasing ability to assume responsibility for himself and thus gain his psychological independence.
>
> (Axline, 1964, p. 48–49)

In order to achieve a state of responsibility the pupils were allotted specific tasks such as setting up the work table and chairs, operating the tape-recorder, 'clearing-up' and ensuring that the puppets were put away in a safe place until the next session. Unlike the clinical therapist who was insistent that Dibs' consultation should only last exactly one hour even when he showed reluctance to go, there was always the temptation to let the group 'over-run' their time through lunch-time motivated as they were by their sheer enthusiasm. Only once did the teacher relent, using the opportunity to discover why the group wanted to stay:

Julian: Miss, what's our next lesson?
Teacher: Well, you're stopping with me aren't you?
Julian: I mean after this 'un.
Teacher: It will be lunch-time (assuming lunch was at midday).
Julian: After this lesson now?
Teacher: Hmm.
Julian: Well, we've got another lesson after this.
Andrew: We an't.
Teacher: No, it's nearly quarter to twelve and then you have another lesson at twelve, but you can stop here can't you?
Julian: Oh great! can we stop here? (Peter's eyes 'light-up')
Teacher: What would you normally have?
Andrew: We have history but ...
Julian: Can we stop here instead for an hour?
Teacher: You can if you like.
Julian: Till dinner-time — shall we stop till dinnertime?
Teacher: There'll be lots of cleaning-up to do anyway, and then you can start thinking about your play can't you? (The bell rings at the end of the lesson)
Julian: Miss, do we go now?
Teacher: Not if you don't want to.
Elaine: I like it best here.
Teacher: Why do you like it best here?
Elaine: I don't like lessons.
Teacher: Why don't you like lessons?
Elaine: They're hard.

Perhaps the decision to let them stay was wrong, as if the teacher was letting the session become an excuse for the group to avoid facing the so-called realities of the subsequent lessons. The decisive factor had been their sheer anxiety of wanting to stay which was so pronounced that the teacher wanted to alleviate their obvious fear of lessons, even though it was only for one brief time each week. The fact that they found lessons difficult could have been the result of a degree of 'fear' or anxiety. It was this episode together with another conversation towards the end of the session which made it for the teacher personally, a very rich and rewarding experience. As the models were nearing completion, the teacher remarked that individuals could help each other to finish:

Teacher:	Peter, perhaps when you've finished entirely Peter could you help Andrew.
Peter:	That's what I'm doing now Miss.
Andrew:	Tha' wain't! He'll ruin it! (jokingly)
Teacher:	He won't give him a chance.
Julian:	Miss, I don't need any help.
Teacher:	Don't you?
Michael:	I don't need any help either Miss.
Andrew:	I don't.
Teacher:	Don't you even want my help?
Michael:	Oh yes Miss, you're different.
Teacher:	Oh, that's alright then.

Not only were the group beginning to respond towards assisting each other, but they were also learning to assert independence, while simultaneously acknowledging the teacher's role as enabler.

Mainly the group was absorbed in the task and the teacher noticed there were long periods where no-one talked. It could be argued that she should have broken these pauses in an attempt to encourage a flow of conversation. While the teacher did comment or ask a leading question, mostly she preferred to wait to provide an opportunity for silences to be broken by other members acting on their own initiative. Furthermore, these respites were periods in which the children tended to relax away from their often excitable state, and began coping with the task of modelling the papier mâché heads. During these sessions of deep concentration, someone might hum a tune or begin to sing gently so that the atmosphere generated a feeling of warmth and intimacy.

Though absorbed concentration was shown, the children's powers of recall were limited; the instructions had to be repeated several times and the group had to be constantly reminded and encouraged as they still liked to know that they were completing the task correctly. Often the teacher wondered whether the reason for this was because her comments and explanations were ambiguous, but equally she observed how individuals seemed 'distant', lost or absorbed in their own thoughts and feelings, only to erupt spasmodically with a mode of speech that assumed the addressee knew the context of their line of thought and could 'home in' as it were, to the meaning. Peter, for example, after talking and singing to his half-made puppet, provides the following discourse:

Peter:	(to puppet) Quack! Quack! (then he sings) They should be banned them!
Julian:	What?

Peter:	'Sex Pistols'. You know what the' sing do they, do you know what they sang once?
Julian:	No, what?
Peter:	(sings) 'God save the Rotten Queen'
Julian:	They're going to be banned aren't they?
Peter:	Yes I know 'cos he is.
	(Pause more singing – do – da – do – la – la – lee, then talks to his puppet in a different voice)
	Hmm, you're a beggar, Jez-a-bel.
Michael:	(holds his puppet to Peter's) Take your partners.

The tune which Peter had been singing stimulated his comment regarding a contemporary pop-group and only when Julian asked 'What?' was further information given in order that Julian could contribute and eventually collaborate with Peter's suggestion that 'they' should be banned. When Julian agrees and confirms, offering definite information 'they're goin to be banned aren't they?', Peter again assumes mutual understanding of the content in his implication that it is only one member that is to be banned 'yes, I know 'cos he is', in this context 'he' could either be the leader of the group or the one who caused adverse publicity. The sequence also illuminates how absorbed Peter and Michael are in creating an animated puppet as they talk and sing to make 'puppet-conversation', investing the puppets with personalities. Michael later becomes amused by Julian who is lulling a tune to his puppet and says 'Julian's been singing a song wi' his puppet' and giggles follow.

While the puppets were capable of having human characteristics endowed on them, so the children invested themselves with features that suggested an identification with the puppet. The following sequence serves to illustrate this observation.

Michael:	Miss, are we making animals or people?
Julian:	People! What else do you think we're making?
Michael:	They're not people though, they are puppets (giggles).
Teacher:	What's the difference between people and puppets?
Michael:	They have strings and we don't.
Teacher:	These haven't got strings they're hand puppets.
Michael:	Miss, these puppets are made by people.
Peter:	Puppets can't talk, puppets can't eat, puppets can't walk, but we can.
Teacher:	Well, last week your puppet 'killed you' do you remember when you held your puppet up and you went 'aah he's killed me'?
Peter:	I don't know what you mean.

Teacher: I mean that you're saying puppets can't talk but I think they can do things.

As the third session concluded Andrew asked if the puppets could be completed in an 'Art and Craft' lesson, or at home and similarly, Peter desired to take his to the 'Communications' lesson. The teacher felt that although she would not be able to record the proceedings, this request was not one to be refused as it suggested interest was permeating into other areas on the curriculum. When the group met for the fourth session the puppets were ready to be used, the next stage being the creation of impromptu dialogues and an improvised play. With the emphasis on simplicity and ingenuity, the 'puppet-theatre' was very fundamental, being an overturned table placed high enough for the children to crouch behind but with sufficient space for movement. Almost immediately the group were hidden behind the screen, they began contributing suggestions for an improvisation based on their earlier ideas.

Andrew: That can be turtle and that can be ... move up!
Michael: PC Copper, I'm the, I'm the wicked wizard Miss ...
Peter: No! You're Policeman Copper.
Michael: I'm a wizard Miss t'policemen don't know where t'robbers are, so they come to see me about it.
Julian: Hello! Can I come in from next door? (knocks with puppet head)
Peter: Pretend you're robbing t'house ...
Julian: Alright.
Peter: An' I'll come out wiv all t'money shuvved under t'here.
Michael: Ged – out – ged – out.
Peter: Then I shoot you, I shoot you, Boo! then you fall dead na — you've gotta fall dead (he pushes the puppet).
Julian: (to Elaine) Come on 'woman' (hee hee).
Peter: No, she's dead, (to puppet) lay there!
Andrew: Let's go for a walk. Aaah!

This illustrates the creative uses of language. It is very similar in form to the role-play that is experienced in improvised drama where the children's play-reality becomes very personalised as they assimilate themselves into a part, 'I shoot you', 'you're robbing t'house', 'I'm the wicked wizard', 'I'll come out wiv all t'money' and 'I'm a constable', are all indications of this. When the teacher intervened, the group temporarily moved from their imaginative play to realising the objectivity of the puppets.

Michael:	I'm a constable Miss.
Teacher:	You're a constable, I thought you were a witch.
Michael:	No Miss, but I've decided to make it into a constable Miss.
Teacher:	Go on then, and then what's yours Peter?
Peter:	Miss he's called 'Spikey' and I'm 'Nosey' and we're robbers.
Teacher:	You're Spikey and Nosey who're robbers, you're the constable (to Michael).
Julian:	I'm a policeman.
Andrew:	An' they — we find all the money and they run away and the policeman starts chasing'em.
Teacher:	Alright, and what about Elaine, what's she going to be?
Elaine:	(holding up the puppet to examine it) It isn't a woman this.
Peter:	It's a grandad.
Michael:	Miss, this can be t'master of disguise whose on, er half of him is on t'er Policeman's side then he decides to go over.

As with the first session where the group displayed an ability to identify with characters sensitively there is a similar ability here. Within the bounds of drama one concern from the teacher's point of view is that which deals with encouraging sensitivity. Perhaps a more accurate term would be 'empathy'.

The sharing or identification of feelings is a particularly important part of successful role-play but it should always be remembered that seeing the world as another does or identifying another person's feelings and problems as if from that point of view will only be temporary, for the main motive is to achieve understanding. In effect, 'empathy' is developing one stage further than the 'willing suspension of disbelief' — the essential involvement which the teacher asks of her pupils in order to create drama. It can be argued that empathy can be acquired and taught. Three phrases of empathy have been described. These are involving the ability to sense the emotions of another person and to communicate this understanding to him or her; the imaginative transposing of oneself into the thinking, feeling and acting of another and so structuring the world as he or she does; finally the ability of putting oneself into the position of a whole class of people. However, it could be added that even if a person can be encouraged rather than taught to understand another's feelings, there is no guarantee that he or she will act upon this information. What impressed the teacher about this group was the apparent ease with which they were able to identify with various roles and with such spontaneity. So far, the teacher was dissatisfied with the superficiality of the progress during this early improvisation, so much so that she expressed her feelings openly to the group: 'so far, we've got a lot of screaming and shouting and not much story'. The difficulty is knowing when to intervene and not only because the teacher felt a rapport with the group could she interrupt as she did. It was a very 'short-sighted' remark to make, because without realising it immediately, the point at which the seemingly 'screaming and shouting' occurred was the moment at which the pupils and puppets became associated together in a mutually creative art; so involved were they in the story that their previous timidity and self-consciousness wavered. It is true, however, that the pupils were hidden behind a screen and were speaking as if they were puppet characters, but with great conviction.

After resuming the plot so far with the group the teacher then temporarily entered the discourse both to broaden the perspective and to obtain a sharper definition.

Teacher: Where has Spike been?
Peter: This one's broken in the house ...
Teacher: Where's the house?
Peter: (pointing to position) Miss, just here.
Teacher: What do you mean, 'just here'? What kind of street is it around?
Peter: Miss er ... Barlborough ... Barlborough Street.
Teacher: Alright then, what has Spike got to say to the other person so that he'll know where to go?
Peter: 'Let's walk up Barlborough Street'.
Teacher: That's better, go on then.
Peter: (turns puppet's head) Hey look!
Teacher: Why don't you have them walking up Barlborough Street? (Peter moves puppet along the table) go on, have them walking up ... right from the other end.
Peter: Hey look Nosey, look up there, look at that house with all the money in.
Andrew: Yes, come on then.
Teacher: Can you see the difference from all that shouting?

To comply with the explicitness the teacher was demanding, required a move from expressive speech to the use of more referential mode, from speech that tells us a good deal about the speaker, his or her feelings and current contributions to the topic, to speech which designates more accurately, refers more superficially and thus communicates to a wider audience. Elements of the language still remained expressive in the sense that it was relaxed, self-presenting and self-revealing, addressed to a few intimate companions, in the sense that it moves easily from general comment to narration of particular experiences and back again, and in the special sense that in making comments, the speakers do not aim at accurate explicit reference in relating experiences, they do not aim at a polished performance. '

The plot began to gain more control and involved two robbers who planned a theft in a house on Barlborough Avenue and who were subsequently arrested and tried. It was a lively and spontaneous effort punctuated by the boys' own attempts to produce sound effects much in the same way as Mark Twain's character in *Tom Sawyer* imitates a steam-boat:

Michael: Do – do – do, do – do – do, do – do – do – do, (walking puppet to the beat of policemen's steps imitating 'Laurel and Hardy').
Peter: Do some glass–window noise–crash.
Michael: Ding – a – ling – a – ling, der – er – er – er (police siren).

There was a request for a third run-through, during which the plot began to develop intricacies as one of the characters decided to 'double cross' his accomplices:

Peter: I'll, I'll shout you, Spike! Spike? Where are you?
Andrew: What?
Peter: Where are you?
Andrew: Here why?
Peter: You know what Jack's told us?
Andrew: Yeh.
Peter: There's a house on bara — barbeque — barber sommat lane.
Andrew: Oh yes, I remember that street, that shop place.
Peter: The house, not the shop, the house you stupid idiot.
Andrew: I'm not a stupid idiot.
Peter: The house I said.
Andrew: Oh ye – ah.
Peter: Come on, half past six OK?
Andrew: Yeh.
Peter: Come on, half past six OK ? OK ! I know what I'll do, I'll go at six o'clock and I'll get more money! I'll get every bit on my own. It's six o'clock now. Constable — there's a constable. He's there get him.
Julian: Ah, Shaddup you fat thing and get him, na – na – na – na
Michael: Someone has taken all the money! Where have they all gone?

Julian: Ah Shaddup.
Peter: Come on Fatty get in.
Michael: It's all right, it's all over.
Peter: No it in't.
Michael: Back to the police-office.
Peter: It's a dummy.
Michael: (fight scene) That's the end children!

Unlike previous sessions where the individuals often spoke at the same time, shouting to gain attention and often completing one another's sentences, this interchange illuminates a gradual awareness of 'other than self', so a more thoughtful exchange is being made. Here Peter and Andrew take their cues from each other and there is a collaboration during which they extend one another's suggestions by further impromptu statements. This can be illustrated for example when Peter cannot remember the name of the street, but Andrew is able to follow on with additional information sufficient to provide Peter with his next lead.

Peter: There's a house on barar — barbeque — barber sommat
        Lane
Andrew: Oh yes, I remember that street, the shop place.
Peter: The house, not the shop, the house you stupid idiot.

A further observation to be made from the extract is the way in which the pace of the spoken word became adjusted to match the assumed audience and the diction of the words has become more carefully pronounced as if the group were aware that more vocal projection is needed when speaking to a wider audience. Still there was evidence of colloquialisms and clichéd responses such as 'stupid idiot', 'all right, it's all over', 'it in't', 'shaddup' but the actual confidence needed to speak was being gained.

The teacher was still concerned that the group should be conscious of the variety of personality traits that their characters could draw from and it was by asking pertinent questions that she was able to guide them towards this during our fifth session:

Teacher: Now what's your character Julian?
Julian: I'm a robber wi' im Miss.
Teacher: What's he called?
Julian: Er, Nosey.
Julian: Er, London.
Teacher: London? Alright what kind of person is he then?
Julian: Thief.
Teacher: Yes, we know he's a thief but what …

Julian:	He's got a posh personality.
Teacher:	How do you mean, a 'posh personality'?
Julian:	Miss, how he talks.
Teacher:	How he talks, alright what must he be thinking at the time of the robbery?

From his earliest reply, Julian understands the term 'character', but when asked 'what kind of a person is he?' it was obvious that the term of reference was obscure. The teacher meant personality, Julian interprets 'kind of person' as role.

Our attention must be alerted to this mis-match of terms of reference and it is for the teacher to phrase the question for it to provide the optimum understanding. Research evidence shows that this is not always true of classroom contexts. Just as when the teacher was about to re-phrase the question to a more open one such as 'What is Nosey like?' or even 'Tell me about your character', Julian volunteered additional information, 'He's got a posh personality.' To obtain a sharper definition, the teacher enquired, 'How do you mean a 'posh personality'?' and Julian's reply 'how he talks' highlights several inferences. An earlier observation had been that the pupils did not listen attentively to each other but vied for attention, giving the impression that they were not sensitive to sounds around them but here Julian shows an awareness of the existing modes and registers of speech different from his own. Furthermore, he feels secure enough to admit his feelings of alienation, and that some people are 'posh'. By inviting him to deduce a reason for why this is so, he adds that it is 'how he talks' that thus categorises people. This could be a contributory underlying reason for such timid children being isolated and experiencing feelings of inferiority. Devaluing a person's language, which is what you do when you accuse it of being inferior, is to devalue the person. It is the meaning potential of a child's language that is important.

Following this exchange a similar depth of insight was offered by Peter after being asked what it was like to feel scared.

Teacher:	What must he be thinking at the time of the robbery?
Julian:	Er, scared.
Teacher:	Scared? What's it like to feel scared? What do you feel scared of? What's it like? ... (to Andrew) What do you feel like when you're scared?
Andrew:	I don't know.
Julian:	Shaking.
Teacher:	Shaking, alright. Do you think that kind of a person would feel shaking then? If he wanted to commit a robbery?

Peter: A robber dun't have time to feel scared, if he saw a ... he
                wasn't checking, he wasn't scared.
Teacher: As he knew what was going to come.

The original question had been what the person must be thinking at
the time, not how he was feeling, yet Julian's reply was an emotional
feeling-response which implies that at this point, this individual at
least, was coming to terms with feelings. Unlike Andrew who
doesn't know or at least couldn't express what such an emotion felt
like, Julian translates his feelings into physical terms — he knows he
experiences 'shaking' when afraid. Peter takes up the discussion
when asked whether or not a person who wanted to commit a
robbery would 'feel shaking'. His reply. 'A robber dun't have time to
feel scared' is more than a broad generalisation, but is a point at which
genuine understanding is reached and parallels the early mentioned
phase of empathy — the ability of putting oneself into the position of a
whole class of people — in this instance, robbers. From the discussion
developed into establishing the fact that the policemen sometimes
'felt scared' but had to be 'brave'.

A contribution from Michael serves to illustrate another characteristic of this exploratory talk, in that when the individuals are
confronted with a challenge that they cannot meet with existing
vocabulary, they use their language creatively to support the answer.

Michael: My name's Constable Jackpot and ...
Teacher: Constable Jackpot?
Michael: My Nick-name's 'Fatty'.
Teacher: Mm ... and how are you different from PC Copper?
Michael: I wear a big hat and he wears a likkle hat.
Teacher: And are you the same kind of.
Michael: I talk Peterbury.
Teacher: Pardon?
Michael: I talk Peterburyish ... I'm from Peterborough.

Obviously the term 'accent' or 'dialect' was not familiar to Michael so to
overcome this he invents the word 'Peterburyish'. Another form of
expression would also be that of gesture in which they tended to motion
with their hands the meaning they were trying to communicate.

When the teacher asked Peter for the details of his character, he was
able to supply a lengthy description which needed little prompting.

Peter: Miss, him? Miss they call him Nosey 'cos all these
                policemen talk about him and he guz up listening, an'
                when he hears women talking about sommat he goes up
                listening again, an' he comes from Birmingham.

Teacher: And how is he different from the other characters you've
got?
Peter: Oh he's, oh, I've forgot his name (now holding second
puppet).
Teacher: He was the … what was he last week? (trying to
remember).
Andrew: He told 'em to do t'jobs.
Teacher: Oh, he was Jack!
Andrew: Jack! he was the one that talked to us an' taught us about
it an' he comes from North America.

The teacher's experience in forgetting one of the character's names
was the same as Peter experienced, and in such a situation, one has
to admit that teachers are not omniscient. Both teacher and pupil
were relying on contributions from the group to remind them,
Andrew supplied the information that this character was the one
who' told 'em to do t'jobs,' from which lead we remembered it was
'Jack'. Provided that such occurrences are genuine, valuable
learning experiences can result because a human setting is made in
which the pupil feels safe enough to explore himself knowing that
someone respects his views. The teacher also observed how Peter
repeated the same phrase 'he guz up' but the second time he tried to
make it less colloquial 'he goes up listening again' as if consciously
experimenting not so much with sound, as his previous 'nick-nack-
nack' sequence showed, but now with various speech registers.

While the boys concerned themselves with the puppet-play,
Elaine assumed a more passive role, preferring to sit next to the
teacher and act as 'audience'. The teacher felt that although she was
evidently enjoying this, it was not really helping her to realise her
own potential in a creative way. This consideration was completely
dismissed during the next session, when Elaine presented the
teacher with a handwritten script which she had made 'so the boys
won't forget what to say'. This marked a stage of achievement, for
while IQ tests and other biographical data coldly banded Elaine into
a 'less able' group, this incident suggests her capabilities when
sufficiently motivated.

It was evident that Elaine needed more opportunity to explore her
latent talents and as the boys had adopted and utilised the glove
puppets and a miniature puppet-theatre with which she could
attempt to create a story using stock characters such as a witch, a
pirate, an indian, a clown and various animals. The teacher left her
alone for a time and soon she related an idea for a story. The theme
centred round two indians who lived on an island and whose only
wealth was a chest of gold. A pirate and sea-captain, accompanied
by a parrot planned to steal the gold but 'Winnie-the-Witch'

knowing of their plan and considering it 'unfair' turns the pirate captain and parrot into a lion, monkey and bear respectively, who subsequently become part of a travelling circus. When, at the end of the interlude Elaine asked if a 'friend' could help her, it appeared that she had been sufficiently motivated in the project to extend it beyond herself and so strengthen relationships with those outside the group. It could be assumed that the product of Elaine's play would be more of fantasy than the boys' had been as it contained all the elements of a good folk-tale, such as good conflicting with evil, retribution, stolen treasure and a journey or quest to find it, but, more fundamentally, the 'touch of magic'.

During the sixth session, not only did Elaine's friend Rosie join the group but also another two appeared, invited by Peter and introduced as 'our sound effects men, Miss' and though the unexpected expansion of the group could have been daunting, the teacher took it as a healthy indication that the project had so far been met with approval and enthusiasm. Whereas in the first session the boys had requested that they 'show' the play to their friends, now they were eager to involve the members of their peer group. During their rehearsal they did not adhere rigidly to Elaine's script but preferred to improvise while still maintaining the overall shape of the plot. This extended their language usage. To do full justice to the play it is best regarded in its entirety in order to appreciate the natural modulation and fluency, as the following short sequence illustrates.

Peter: (N)	Do you know who's back from America?
Julian: (S)	Who?
Peter: (N)	Jack.
Julian: (S)	Who's our Jack?
Peter: (N)	Jack that taught us how to burgle houses tha' knows. Look he's here (other puppet appears). Hello Jack!
Peter: (J)	Hi there (pause) I want you to do this house, see it over t'hill, it's up Barber Street, can you see it?
Julian: (S)	Yes, what time?
Peter: (N)	What tonight? Half past six tonight OK?
Julian: (S)	OK, Jack.
Peter: (N)	Fine, on the dot! We're just going for a drink and a chat (puppets exit except 'Spike').
Julian: (S)	I know, I'll go at six o'clock and then I will burgle on my own (making crashing sound, robs house) Jack! Jack!

(S) — Spike; (N) — Nosey; (J) — Jack.

One interesting facet of the rehearsal was that when a particular scene had been played, the boys changed roles so each was given an opportunity to portray various characters, thus extending relation-ships and their view of 'fair-play'. Throughout this practice it was noticed how the boys varied their voices to extend the role they were enacting. Michael, for example, as policeman often deepened and thickened his voice, and Peter, while manipulating two puppets, varied his accordingly.

Michael: (deepened voice) Oh yes you're coming for a likkle ride wiv us.
Peter: Why don't you get Nosey and Jack, they're gone into the house (piping tone) don't get me, it wasn't me!

Similarly, Elaine reminds Rosie that 'we can't do it in our voices though.'

When the boys were satisfied with the sequence of the play and having mastered sound effects, the teacher asked simply what they 'wanted to do with the play', and immediately Andrew suggested 'show it to some likkle 'uns'. Julian also thought that if we showed the play to the 'whole school we can charge a penny for charity'. This was reminiscent of his idea after the first session in which he had been keen to act as publicity manager and to make posters and tickets for the venture. Though the teacher had not anticipated this development, the suggestions in themselves implied the extent to which the confidence within the group was being extended. It was arranged for the group to visit a local infant school where they could present their play and the procedure was recorded on video. The setting was itself improvised, but the makeshift resources were utilised to their best possible advantage.

As a performance, the results were disappointing. As the boys were eager and apprehensive, their obvious tension conveyed a very trite plot, and the quality of the recording tended to be static because of the cramped conditions. It was the experience itself and subsequent development which was rewarding. This development occurred during the girls' presentation when a most striking thing happened, for in addition to addressing the audience with the pre-planned 'Hello, boys and girls', Elaine invited the audience to accompany the witch in 'weaving the magic spells'.

This 'flight' from the script is an accepted event which influences many performers who intuitively feel the audience reaction or their anticipated response and so spontaneously mould and adapt their performance accordingly. Such a decision takes great courage and confidence as the result could be disastrous should the response not be favourable. Within the scope of a puppet-play, it could be that the child works out an adjustment to the world as he or she finds it. The puppet, so the child feels, dominates the situation and the child has a feeling of power in being able to control his or her audience, his or her outside world. This in itself is a great help in confidence-building. Audience-participation is such that in the girls' presentation the puppet-to-audience relationship increased rapport with the children, eased tension and broke down resistance. So completely does the child — both the operator and audience — enter into this new world of relationships that it is important to ease the adjustment back to reality. In order to do this, members of the infant audience were invited to come behind the puppet-theatre to try manipulating them and attempting an impromptu play. The young children were eager to co-operate, but their tentativeness at speaking other than in monosyllables or phatic salutations such as 'Hello', served to highlight the contrast between them and the actual group with whom the teacher had been working. One of the disadvantages of working closely on such a project is that the ability to assess or evaluate progress or development is difficult until a contrast or comparison is created. Here, the infants' first attempts at impromptu dialogue were reminiscent of the boys' earlier attempts and yet when working on the project, the boys had gained a confidence which came to fruition, through the creation and presentation of the puppet-play. So much of the language experience offered to children with special language needs, is split off from any personal engagement in living which denies the learners' (and the teacher's) creative engagement in learning.

SUMMARY

The expressive arts such as dance, drama, music, film and puppetry, have an important place within English studies. Children with special needs have been found to benefit from a broad curriculum such as an arts-based approach to English would allow. By dwelling too much on alleged 'basics' in terms of spelling, punctuation, handwriting, reading schemes and other 'packages' in English studies, we deny our pupils a creative expression of experience. But if we intend to work from fundamental 'basics', then we cannot avoid one basic truth about the acquiring of language: that living language is interwoven with living being.

In Conclusion: Open Up

I think that if a lesson is boring you don't tend to listen. It is just like watching a very slow snail sliding up a garden path. If a particular lesson is really boring you might think it would be more interesting watching a tree grow.

(Tracey: aged 14)

Teaching pupils with special needs is not easy. Many, like Tracey, seemed bored with what is on offer at school. The class teacher, frustrated by class sizes, lack of support and meagre resources, similarly feels at a loss at what to do for the best as the range of pupils with special needs is so widespread. On the one hand, some pupils are timid and withdrawn, indeed 'shut up' within themselves. Then there are those boisterous, more demanding pupils whose behavioural difficulties force the teacher to tell them to 'shut up'. Pupils at both ends of the spectrum experience a degree of difficulty in communication. Such pupils lack sufficient self-confidence to form learning relationships in a creative way. It is easier too for the teacher to 'cope' if she presents her class with various ready-made, pre-packaged schemes of work designed to keep everybody quiet and safe, for the teacher's own confidence may have gradually become undermined, so she does not work creatively.

It is only by gaining self-respect through a mutually trusting relationship that individuals become valued and self-accepting. This in turn becoms extended to relationships with others so that individuals gain respect and accept others as they are with a belief in their capacities. With a permissiveness to utilise these capacities, the individual assumes a responsibility for making decisions. This is a real belief in the integrity of the individual which places emphasis on a positive and creative way of life.

Such consideration is true of any learning relationship. Where classroom relationships are concerned, the element of complete acceptance of the pupil seems to be of such vital importance. It is an acceptance of the belief that the pupil has the ability to be a feeling, thinking, independent, creative human being. It is also an understanding of that never-ceasing drive towards self-realisation or complete fulfilment of the self as an individual. Whereas an adjusted child grows without encountering too many difficulties or obstacles in her path, pupils with special needs are initially denied the right to achieve this maturity without a struggle.

The approach with these pupils has to be outgoing starting from where the individual is. The establishing of a warm, friendly atmosphere can be likened to many similar situations within the field of dynamic psychology; for example what Axline had to say has the same relevance now:

> In the warm and friendly relationships which the counsellor establishes the client is enabled to face himself squarely, feeling secure in this genuinely co-operative relationship, experiencing an absolute togetherness in this effort to achieve complete self-understanding and self-acceptance.
>
> (Axline, 1947, p. 97)

So the building up of a 'good-enough' working relationship based on mutual trust and respect is the first essential. For the teacher to be creative in the full sense and to develop a creative curriculum for her pupils means that she must know the pupils well enough to discern their immediate needs and to anticipate their long-term needs. It requires her being able to recognise and to enrich a 'cultural playground' which would allow learning to take place.

ARTS EXPERIENCE AS CENTRAL TO THE EDUCATION OF CHILDREN WITH SPECIAL NEEDS

Throughout the previous sections, it has been demonstrated that the difficulty children encountered in their language and learning relationships are mainly emotional ones. Arts experience is essential for emotional growth, yet arts experience, especially that of poetry, is a neglected part of the curriculum for children with special needs.

In a modest paper 'Poetry in Remedial Classes', Gregory (1967) gave similar consideration, though his view, not being followed by rigorous research, did not receive the serious attention or readership it deserved. His opening paragraph was indeed memorable:

> I think it it axiomatic that we teach poetry at any level for at least two reasons: to pass on to our pupils their cultural inheritance, and because it is pleasant and gives pleasure. The second reason may not be quite distinct from the first, and if we were to analyse it more carefully we would probably find that part of the pleasure it gives is due to the strengthening effect that makes this, and the other arts, particularly useful allies in remedial teaching, in the development of that all-important relationship between teacher and pupil without which nothing happens.
>
> (Gregory, 1967, pp. 33–35)

Through admitting the crucially generative presence of emotion in poetry, we begin to realise a basic insight into the nature of the learning process itself — that there is only valid learning where there is emotional contact between teacher and observed world, between teacher and learner, between learner and observed world, between learner and learner. By considering that the difficulties of the disaffected pupil is partly an emotional problem, and that healthy emotional growth is bound up with the quality of a person's expressive life, then arts experience, with its stronghold in the emotions, can be seen to be the means through which the pupils emotional needs are satisfied.

To recall again the difficulties encountered by Tom Brangwen, what we recognise is a child who is panicked by 'deliberate learning' and then assailed by the emotional impact of a poem:

> But he loved anyone who could convey enlightenment to him through feeling. He sat betrayed with emotion when the teacher of literature read, in a moving fashion, Tennyson's *Ulysses*, or Shelley's *Ode to the West Wind*. His lips parted, his eyes filled with a strained, almost suffering light. And the teacher read on, fired by his power over the boy. Tom Brangwen was moved by this experience beyond all calculation, he almost dreaded it, it was so deep. But when, almost secretly and shamefully, he came to take the book himself, and began the words 'Oh wild west wind, thou breath of autumn's being', the very fact of the print caused a prickly sensation of repulsion to go over his skin, the blood came to his face, his heart filled with a bursting passion of rage and incompetence. He threw the book down and walked over it and went out to the cricket field. And he hated books as if they were his enemies. He hated them worse than ever he hated any person.
>
> He could not voluntarily control his attention. His mind had no fixed habits to go by, he had nothing to get hold of, nowhere to start from. For him there was nothing palpable, nothing known in himself, that he could apply to learning. He did not know how to begin. Therefore he was helpless when it came to deliberate understanding or deliberate learning.
>
> (Lawrence, 1915, pp. 16–17)

Tom was at the mercy of feelings to which he could not give any coherence. Significantly, too, his sense of failure with the mechanical schoolwork which the poem interrupts is increased. He feels even more helpless in the face of the demands of 'deliberate understanding' — the mechanically argumentative discourse which leaves him convinced 'He was a fool' (Lawrence, 1915, p. 16).

Within the area of 'special needs' the primary need of individuals is for a sense of meaning in their lives which they realise through symbolism. This view accords well with the opinions of Post-Kantian philosophers Cassirer (1944) and Langer (1942) for example, who believed that many problems in our studies of the human being and society are solved more readily if we regard man as the 'animal symbolicum'. The work of the British psychiatrist Winnicott substantiated this (Winnicott, 1958). He found that disturbed people could not begin to work towards recovery until they confronted the question: 'Who am I?' He maintained that it is through cultural symbolism that the human being comes to terms with this question. The development of the capacity to symbolise, and the engagement with culture are primarily imaginative activities. In the light of these insights, imagination is the very basis of our effectiveness in dealing with the world, and attention to the need to symbolise is at the centre of a child's learning.

All children have the ability to use language imaginatively: yet with children who are experiencing difficulties in learning, the danger may be that we shy away from helping them with their own symbol-making in favour of a sterile curriculum made up mainly of 'compensatory language programmes' devoid of anything that will encourage the expression of experience through the symbolic use of words. Carefully selected patterns of work designed to meet the needs of the child must take priority over the superficial, threadbare and mediocre round of exercises, comprehension tests, and reading schemes so popular in many English and remedial departments for use with children who are said to have 'special needs' where their language is their cause for concern. There can be no justification for offering that which is spurious; rather we must genuinely create a classroom culture where the poetic spirit can be nurtured; indeed, the body of poetry that we make accessible to pupils with learning difficulties is surely the most comprehensive 'language development programme' that is available.

But how can we recover an element of 'play' in learning in order that children who are experiencing difficulties may instead become engaged in learning as a pleasurable act? How can we help the pupils to make living connections with texts often considered 'too difficult'?

Much of what I am suggesting as an approach to teaching children with learning difficulties can be summarised at this point in Ian McMillan's poem entitled *Child's Guide to Ian McMillan* (it belongs to the poet's private collection and is as yet unpublished):

> look look
> who is this
> this is ian
> ian ian
> this is ian
> see ian

look look
what is ian doing
oh oh
ian is writing
i see ian writing
write write ian
ian is writing
what is ian writing
ian is writing a poem
poem poem
poem poem
see ian write the poem

look look
who is this
this is ian's friend
hello friend
hello hello
look look

what is ian's friend doing
he is reading ian's poem
read read
see the friend read

listen listen
what are ian and his friend doing
they are talking
talk talk talk talk
ian and his friend are talking

listen listen
what is ian's friend saying
he is saying
i don't get it
i don't understand your poem

listen listen
what is ian saying
he is saying
my poem means this this this
my poem means this

listen listen
what is ian's friend saying
he is saying
why didn't you say so?
I thought it meant that, that that
I thought it meant that

listen listen
ian is shouting
shout, shout shout

It means this, it means this,
    it means this
see ian shouting

look look
what are ian and his friend
    doing
they are fighting

fight fight
biff biff
pow pow
bam splat
zowie oof
oof zowie

what strange noises
see all the blood
blood bones and teeth

here come the policemen
arrest arrest
here comes the ambulance
white white white white

here come the policemen
arrest arrest

here comes the press
picture picture

here come the headlines
shock shock / row row / poet poet /
    disgust

it is disgusting poets week
    in the sun

where is the poem

lost lost the poem is lost

This piece by a respected contemporary South Yorkshire poet,
parodies the mechanical style prevalent in the early reading
schemes for pupils; the same mechanical schoolwork with which

Tom Brangwen felt a failure. At the same time, McMillan's piece points to the direction of a curriculum for children with learning difficulties — that of allowing them to write and talk about their own experiences and personal symbol-making. It hints at the shift from private to public worlds. It also conveys a sense of the pupils' sharing and exploring texts in order to establish meaning; yet there is also the echoing truth of how English teachers are seen to be keepers of the key to unlocking the 'Pandora's Box' of right answers, rather than allowing the children to discover meanings for themselves. The climax of the piece reveals that within our curriculum for pupils with learning difficulties, we can pose and answer the question: 'Where is the poem? lost lost the poem is lost'.

Every true language lesson can only be a creative act both for the pupil and for the teacher when the authority of arts expression as a central and essential mode of insight in creative intellectual thinking and living is allowed to be dominant. What follows is how the teacher grappled with this problem and sought to find an alternative way to share a text with a group of children said to be 'remedial'. The diary extracts first of all indicate that an earlier attempt, largely based on a more traditional model of presenting poetry to a class, proved to be unsuccessful:

21st October
I presented 5C with *Limbo* by Seamus Heaney this morning — the one which tells of the drowning of an illegitimate baby who is netted along with a catch of salmon by fishermen at Ballyshannon. After reading the poem to them, it was clear from the group's response that they were confused by it, thinking for example that the baby was a fish. How can I help them to understand the stark imagery in the metaphor 'he was a fish tearing her open'?

25th October
We looked again more closely at the poem *Limbo* by Seamus Heaney but I approached this in a different way using first a selection of prints and photographs mainly around the theme of birth. These included: *Le Berceau* (Berthe Morisot); *Young Woman on the Beach* (Edvard Munch); *The Tragedy,* and *The Fisherman's Farewell* (Pablo Picasso).

I had also selected some pictures showing human embryonic development. The pictures were circulated between friendship groups and some of the talk was recorded.

In larger groups, the poem was looked at again, and this time, the response was much more satisfying. When I joined in the talk with one group for example, I asked, 'Where in the poem is the baby said to be *like* a fish?' There was little point in using the words 'metaphor' and 'imagery' but nevertheless encouraging a response that would draw upon this idea. Michael suggested 'he was a minnow' was a possibility, then John — probably the weakest in the group — added

'Yeh, it sounds like they meant the baby was live bait'. His remark was interesting for several reasons. John had stumbled on and formed his own metaphor which encompassed Heaney's imagery of fishing developed throughout the poem — 'he was a minnow', 'illegitimate spawning', 'a small one thrown back', 'he was hauled in' and 'netted an infant'. His reply suggested too, that John considered the infant to be still alive when it had been put into the water which has far wider moral implications than if the baby had been initially dead; Heaney only implies this with the phrase 'ducking him tenderly'. John had actually understood quite a bit about the poem without any conscious help from the teacher.

Not all pupils can respond to a text with such confidence and the support of the teacher needs to be sustained for those pupils who are finding it difficult initially to engage with a text. In the following transcripts of the same lesson, the teacher now guides the pupils through the poem following their rhythms of response:

Teacher: What do you think's happening here? What's been thrown into the water?
Gina: Oh! They're fishing.
Teacher: They're fishing in the water — yes — Mm.
Cordelia: Nets.
Teacher: Yes — what did they bring up? What did they get?
Yasmin: Catch.
Teacher: And what else? Second line ...
Mark: Salmon.
Patrick: Infant.
Teacher: Yes — so what's happened? What's the poem about? (reads part of poem) 'Fishermen at Ballyshannon /Netted an infant last night / Along with the salmon ...'
Patrick: They've picked a body up.
Teacher: Mm — What — What body?
Gina: Baby.
Patrick: Likkle baby.

After bringing the narrative into focus, a more conjectural discussion is developed:

Teacher: Yes and how did it (the baby) get there do you think?
Patrick: Somebody might have hidden there and threw it in or it — it might have been on t'edge and it's fell in.
Teacher: So who do you think the 'she' is — in the second verse?
Patrick: Could have been a girl.
Teacher: Mm — and what do we know about the baby? (pause)

Gina: Small.
Teacher: Small. Mm — Is there anything to tell you how it got there?
Cordelia: It says: 'a small one thrown back'.
Teacher: Alright yes — so who's — who's put it in the water then?
Gina: The ...
Teacher: The ... ?
Cordelia: She has. Mm ... why?
Yasmin: She can't look after it.
Teacher: Why? Why would someone — a woman — put a baby in the water and drown it?
Darren: She might not want it.
Teacher: Mm — why not?
Gina: Her parents — parents might have told her she can't have it.

It is always tempting for the teacher to rush in and ask questions: by doing so, she often discourages pupils from active learning through exploratory talk. The reflecting indicated by prefaces such as 'might have' and 'could have', allows time for silences where ideas are formulated. In this example, the teacher's relaxed and unhurried involvement prompts the pupils to reshape their earlier confusion into a coherence through a shared encounter both with each other and with the text. As more confidence is gained, a feeling of empathy with the mother becomes apparent as the group move towards making the text become their own.

Teacher: Alright — does she feel like doing this? Does she want to do it?
Darren: No.
Teacher: Can you find any lines which tell us that? That she didn't particularly want to?
Yasmin: Tenderly.
Teacher: Tenderly — good.
Gina: 'Tearing her open'.
Teacher: Yes what was it really? What does that mean?
Gina: In fact — when she was doing it she was crying.
Teacher: Possibly. Mm — what is the er — baby compared with? What's it compared with all the time?
Yasmin: Fish.

The group begin to identify with the central character: 'in fact — when she was doing it she was crying'. The teacher is guiding their understanding of the poem by gently probing their responses and leading them to form others. Another movement develops when the discourse moves on to more universal themes only possible after the teacher had helped the pupils to be aware of a feeling-response through unravelling with them the complexities of the poem, both in terms of its meaning and its structure, its feelings and its intentions:

Teacher: Whose baby is it though?
Darren: Fishes.
Teacher: Whose is it? Whose baby is it? It's hers isn't it? It's hers because on line 4 what does it say about it?
Yasmin: It's illegitimate.
Teacher: That it was illegitimate wasn't it? So does that give any clues as to why she wanted to drown the baby?
Yasmin: It didn't have a father.
Teacher: Mm — and do you think that's important that people have a mother and a father or is it more acceptable to have an unmarried mother these days?
Patrick: Yeh — so long as you love it.

One could be at first puzzled by Darren's response that the baby belongs to the fishes until recalling the myths of the fisher-king. From this, the discourse moves to a consideration of illegitimacy and its acceptability in society with the group concluding that it does not really matter whether the baby has one or two parents 'so long as you love it.' The empathy that they earlier felt for the main protagonist in the poem is thus transferred towards the lived world of real people. This is further developed when the group finally bring the poem and their own lives into relation with each other as a more personal sharing of experience is disclosed:

Gina: Our Maxine's having a baby in four month.
Teacher: What's she hoping for?
Gina: She wants a little boy.
Teacher: Does she? What's she going to call him?
Gina: I don't know.
Teacher: Will you be an aunty then?
Gina: Mm.
Teacher: Lovely.
Patrick: My aunty's just had a babby.
Teacher: Alright. What I'd ... (then realising Patrick's comment) Oh! Has she?
Patrick: My aunty — it's called Brian.
Teacher: Brian is it?
Patrick: Me sister's called hers Oliver.

The nature of the talk is intimate as the group exchanges personal experiences. After talking about the poem, the group were invited to give a written response. Patrick attempts to convey the pain of childbirth and the mother's relief when finally 'a scream is heard':

> An unborn baby is waiting
> for the mother has been in
> pain. It seems like years
> more, those months of waiting.
>
> Inside, the mother can feel
> it moving about, from side to side
> up and down.
> If she is quiet, she can hear it.
>
> As she gets closer to having it,
> the pains get worse
> and worse. It is only very tiny
> about six inches high.
>
> The water is swishing about, all
> around the baby. The little heart
> is beating very fast
> and is very little.
>
> It is placed in a black
> hole, curled up tight and sucking
> its thumb. It wants
> to be born.
>
> The mother's pain is harder
> and she knows it is
> wanting to be born. Its
> mother gets very nervous.
>
> Her waters burst. The pain
> gets worse and worse. She
> feels like she
> cannot go through with it.
>
> Throughout the theatre
> a scream is heard.
> At last it is born
> It is a little boy.

In this piece, Patrick gives a detailed account of a birth probably drawing his source of reference from overheard conversations at home and through describing some of the pictures that the teacher has brought in, but the connecting and reflecting is Patrick's own personal activity.

In contrast, Gina manages to convey economically, the emotional rather than the physical pain at the birth of a stillborn child:

> Inside the mother's womb
> Warm and quiet
> Surrounded by darkness
> Unknown to the world
> All is dark
> Not a mumble or a twitch
> The mother feeling heavy
> A stone curled up inside
> She wonders where the kick has gone.

Gina's is not a living stone but a heaviness which makes the mother wonder 'where the kick has gone'.

It does not necessarily follow that the second approach used by the teacher will help to make the poem meaningful to everyone in the group. Darrren is still unsure:

Teacher: Did you like that poem? What did you think about it?
Darren: Yeh.
Gina: It was alright.
Darren: It didn't make sense.
Teacher: Why didn't it make sense?
Yasmin: Darren — a poem doesn't make sense.
Darren: It does — it *should* do.
Yasmin: Does not.
Darren: Should.
Yasmin: Should not.
Darren: Should.
Yasmin: Should not though (others in the group laugh at this).

Perhaps Darren and Yasmin were enjoying nothing more than a playful squabble during which they play with the sound of their own voices. But haven't we all at some stage admitted the same bewilderment: that a poem was difficult to comprehend at first? Often as teachers, our own self-doubt results in us making poetry more mystifying for our pupils. If we regard poetry as being 'too hard' for children with learning difficulties, then we are guilty of anticipating a reaction from them similar to that of Alice — 'I'm afraid I don't understand'. And aren't we then tempted to adopt Humpty Dumpty's overbearing attitude that 'it gets easier further on'? Had this teacher, taking her cue from Darren that the poem 'didn't make sense', abandoned her presentation of poetry, many of the group would not have become actively involved in their own symbol-making. They too like Yasmin and Darren would be resigned to the idea that 'a poem doesn't make sense'. Instead, the task which faced the teacher was to find ways in which Yasmin and Darren could make meaning through their own talking about the experience.

TOWARDS A CREATIVE CURRICULUM

The basic principles of client-centred therapy seem to have far-reaching implications for educators and to hold good when working with pupils who have special needs. One reason for this is that dynamic psychology, unlike many aspects of the educational curriculum, is concerned with the development of self-expression. The single factor in learning which is most often over-looked in the learning process, is the relationship that is built up between the teacher and her pupils. This holds true whether one's approaches are traditional or progressive: it is the permissiveness to be themselves, the understanding and acceptance, the recognition of feelings, the clarification of what they feel and think, that helps children retain their self-respect and the possibility of growth and change which are forthcoming as they develop insight. These conditions set the scene for the teacher to use his or her skills whereby the pupils can fulfil their potential.

An atmosphere of warmth and friendliness on the part of the teacher will establish the type of rapport between herself and a pupil that will seem to individualise the learning even though there are other pupils in the class. The pupil will be accepted exactly as he or she is. By establishing a feeling of permissiveness in the relationship, the pupil feels free to express his or her feelings and to be his or herself. This is easy to say but not as easy to carry through in the classroom. A word of caution can be included here, for unlike the therapeutic relationship where the child expresses his or her feelings completely without restraint, in class, necessary limits are needed to be placed on complete expression of feeling, so some 'protective' perimeter can be included so that the value of releasing feelings is projected through tangible, creative expression be it exploratory talk, drama, art, music, writing or puppetry.

Unlike the cool, detached or even neutral relationship associated with some therapeutic contexts, the teacher becomes a facilitator, providing a realistic and human setting in which pupils feel safe enough to explore their true selves. In the emotional warmth of a relationship individuals experience a feeling of safety as they find that whatever attitude they express will be understood, and their frame of reference perceived with acceptance and respect. If pupils with special needs learn to communicate with and trust one adult, then the hope is that they could feel confident to do this again in other relationships. The crucial factor throughout should be the creation of an atmosphere of mutual trust and respect together with flexibility in which the pupils can explore the truth about their capabilities and relationships. In many respects, the classroom is then similar to that of the therapeutic 'holding' of a patient. Lomas explained that:

> a milieu and medium is provided in which the patient can give up his pretences of functioning adequately and can explore, imagine and develop rather in the way in which a baby can grow in the presence of a mother, who supports but does not unduly impinge.
>
> (Lomas, 1973, p. 142)

The value of this concept of 'holding' when applied to learning is that children in learning attachments need a protective care which will allow them to 'be' and grow. These children need psychological, social and emotional space to grow. In such a context, there will be certain moments in the developing relationship of trust in which the teacher and pupil will feel a corresponding emotional response and will act upon it spontaneously. This will extend to the class-room culture as a whole when the teacher, immediately and intuitively sensing the mood of the class, will then select her material to match that feeling response.

By accepting Winnicott's model of 'good-enough' mothering as the basis for our consideration of the pupil–teacher relationship, then we have to recognise that what counts before anything else is the emotional quality of that relationship. Extending this model into the teacher–pupil relationship implies that nothing is possible outside a relationship of trust between teacher and pupil, qualities that are generated through the experience of personal interaction. The mother and child play together, only when the actual relationship between them in terms of their mutual interdependence of the role has been established, tested and found secure.

A creative curriculum relies upon the initiative taken by the teacher in establishing a good-enough relationship with the pupils. It requires the teacher to get to know her pupils and to devise experiences that will allow the development of trust through these experiences. This phase of the encounter I take to be analogous to the first two stages of Winnicott's sequence of 'good-enough' mothering, the object of which is the separating off of the not-me from me. This sequence comprises holding, handling and object presenting; Winnicott explained:

> A baby is held, and handled satisfactorily, and with this taken for granted is presented with an object in such a way that the baby's

legitimate experience of omnipotence is not violated. The result can be that the baby is able to use the object, and to feel as if this object is a subjective object, and created by the baby.

All this belongs to the beginning, and out of all this comes the immense complexities that comprise the emotional and mental development of the infant and child.

(Winnicott, 1971, p. 131)

The teacher is able to generate a comparable sense of confidence and trustworthiness through her interaction with the pupil. The 'holding' and 'handling' will be emotional bonds rather than also physical as in the mother–baby interaction, but the effect is to free the child from apprehension and to open her to comprehension. Knowing the pupil also means knowing what the pupil is ready for in terms of learning experiences. The teacher must be able to discern and enter upon the stage the pupil is at. This does not mean that a teacher needs to know the intimate details of every pupil's life and background, but to be aware of them may be necessary with some individuals. Rather the teacher needs to be able to 'place' broadly the pupil in terms of the group's general expressive development, to know his or her characteristic modes of organising experience.

Such an approach enables the teacher to stimulate creative changes by beginning with the psychodynamics of the individual, starting where the individual is. Knowing the pupil gives way to knowing the environment, that is, the medium through which expressive knowing is to be effected. Just as it is the mother's task to provide the child with media through which the separation in consciousness of not-me from me might be effected (Winnicott's third phase 'object-presenting'), so it is the teacher's task to select appropriate representational media to facilitate particular learning experiences. The teacher provides the pupils with situations, experiences and materials that are appropriate to their stage of development and which will set them reaching forward for solutions and new understandings. Maslow made the point about the impact upon us of our personal environment:

The communication relationship between the person and the world is a dynamic one of mutual forming and lifting – lowering of each other, a process that we may call 'reciprocal isomorphism'. A higher order of persons can understand a higher order of knowledge, but also a higher order of environment tends to lift the level of the person, just as a lower order of the environment tends to lower it. They make each other more like each other. These notions are also applicable to the interrelations between persons, and should help us to understand how persons help to form each other.

(Maslow, 1975, p. 56)

Applying Maslow's comments to the classroom, the necessity for an enriching classroom environment where the learner is encouraged to make living connections cannot be over-emphasised. When considering pupils with special needs, such an enriching curriculum has to be re-established, as provision for these pupils tends to be impoverished in terms of their arts experience. Maslow also stressed the importance of relationships within such an environment and this has been reiterated by Ross (1978) who commented that a 'good-enough' teacher will always have a life-enhancing effect upon her pupils. The pupils need to feel that the teacher is there alongside them, on the inside of experience as it were, sensitive to the pressures and tensions, ready with suggestions with emotional and intellectual support at the right moment. It is a dynamic role which changes its form as the teacher and pupil adapt to meet the changing needs of their relationship.

Whereas a therapist may be necessary to release blocks in development, the teacher works with healthy, vital forces and nurtures them into fully mature functioning. It is essentially a difference of emphasis: the roles are closely linked and, especially when working with children who are experiencing learning difficulties, the roles at times overlap. Enrichment is achieved by presenting the pupils with a climate where teacher and pupil dare to be creative rather than skulking in patterns of teaching that have been designed to 'keep them quiet for half an hour'. Language is the means through which this enrichment is celebrated. We develop language as we develop life: life generates language. Included in this experience of being alive is the very experiencing of the creative process itself: creativity, in the way Winnicott (1971) used it, is the state of individual living. The teacher is responsible for providing for her pupils the thing that language points to: the rich poem; the engaging story, and especially for children with special needs the opportunity for exploratory talk. In this way, the development of a living language is an organic process and a bodily encounter through the relationships within a given group. Such encounter emerges through patterns of talk. There is an inseparable bond in human talk, between human relationships and what is actually said. The following description of a healthy classroom climate focuses on this bond:

> The range of language which will be permitted within the classroom when one allows it to become more like a gathering of friends is likely to be far wider than often allowed at present, for in an atmosphere of mutual trust between friends there is a willingness to be tentative, open and mutually supportive, which will occasion language that will be elliptical, bantering, colloquial, hesitating but always relaxed … Expressive talk relies upon an interest in the speaker, as well as

in what he is saying, and therefore assumes an interest in a human
being as human being.

(Stratta, Dixon and Wilkinson, 1973, p. 172)

It is this very 'interest in a human being as human being' that a
'good-enough' teacher–learner relationship depends upon. When a
teacher respects the dignity of her pupils and treats them with
understanding, kindliness and gives constructive help, she is
developing in them the ability to look within themselves for the
answer to their problems and to become responsible for them as
independent individuals in their own right. Growth is a gradual
process which cannot be hurried, only anticipated. It comes from
within the individual and cannot be imposed by force from without
but it can be either nurtured or starved by the environment. It is the
relationship between the teacher and her pupils that is the
important consideration in the process of the learner's growth. This
should not be a parasitic dependence, for then the forces within turn
to false independence. The individual needs to be given the sense of
his or her own value and the sense that there are others whom he or
she can trust. Within this relationship there is the value of catharsis
— the outpouring and purging of the emotions, but the addition of
reflecting feelings and total acceptance are the added elements that
help the pupil to clarify feeling which will develop insight.

There is a parallel between the 'good-enough' mother and the
'good-enough' teacher relationship here. In attending to her baby's
emotional needs, the mother learns to create a 'safety-zone' round
herself in which the child can show her hesitancy as well as her
daring; this, as Hourd (1951, p. 68) pointed out, is 'a place where
there is room for advance and retreat to find their own rhythm'. So
much of our learning is dependent upon these patterns, and the
teacher too needs to create zones of safety.Within this safety-zone,
the child gradually gains the confidence to 'expand into language'.
For the developing person, language is 'Lebensraum', the living
space. To be gentle and undignified with children, is to have the
true dignity of adulthood which seeks neither to impress nor
exploit, but only to help children to grow in this living space.
Recognition of special needs follows naturally from such attitudes.

The teacher's response must meet the needs of the pupils she
teaches, but not just the material needs of reading and writing. A
curriculum that is worthy of a place in our educational system
provides an opportunity to enrich the pupil's life far beyond the
academic requirements. Limitation of growth is not confined to the
intellectual sphere. Feelings are complex and in order for them to
exist with full intensity they need an environment where they can
flourish such as only the arts can provide. (The School Curriculum

Development Committee's 'Arts in Schools Project' holds possibilities here. One of its main areas, with which the present writer is involved (Walsh, 1988), is concerned with the arts and children with special needs.)

True education does not neglect these critical emotional needs of the individual, rather it educates the emotions by gently discouraging cliché and by getting pupils to respond as individuals. Such an education encourages pupils to live more deliberately through the senses, thus taking reality in directly as feeling quality, not filtering it through the grid of second-hand concepts and ideas. The movement is towards 'first-hand experiencing' and direct feeling – contact with reality undertaken with great sensitivity and careful regard for the pupils' capacities.

In this respect, the teacher is more than a dispenser of facts and a tester of accumulated knowledge, rather she has an obligation to develop sufficient insight, understanding and interest in the human beings that come before her, so that they will know not only subject matter but themselves and others a little better. It calls for serenity and a ready sense of humour to create or restore a relaxed atmosphere. The teacher then lets the love of her subject show in her outward demeanour. She needs to have a steady affection for her pupils and a respect for all those entrusted in her care, in the full knowledge that affective development cannot take place in the face of hostility or indifference. Only then will the pupils each experience a feeling of personal value and dignity, not simply as pupils without achievements to their credit, but as the valued individuals they are. Pupils with special needs can only gradually come to accept themselves if they feel valued and respected and if their dignity is not threatened.

The teacher can only encourage the feeling of personal worth in her pupils if she is herself emotionally generous and willing to impart her own vitality to her pupils without fearing to reveal her true self. Above all, we need to learn in education how to recapture simplicity. This does not mean that there is at any time a lessening or licence of educational standards, it is rather merely pointing to the fact that the individual, to be truly educated, must be considered a unique person, entitled to respect and understanding and the opportunity to develop to his or her fullest capacities with confidence. Only authentic personal relationships which recognise the humanness of us all, can permit and encourage spontaneity and growth. The realness that we as teachers offer to our children is one that includes a caring, trust and respect for the learner; only in this way can the climate for learning be enhanced. A sensitivity and empathy towards the learner creates a freeing environment which encourages self-initiated learning and growth: the child is trusted to develop. Being responsive to the needs of our pupils is to respect the uniqueness of the other and to help them to unfold, and flourish.

References and Suggestions for Further Reading

Abbs, P. (1982) *English Within the Arts: A Radical Alternative for English and the Arts in the Curriculum*. London: Hodder and Stoughton.

Axline, V. (1947) *Play Therapy*. Massachusetts: Ballantyne.

Axline, V. (1964) *Dibs: In Search of Self*, Harmondsworth: Penguin.

Barnes, D. (1976) *From Communication to Curriculum*. Harmondsworth: Penguin.

Barnes, D. and Barnes, D. (1984) *Versions of English*. London: Heinemann.

Barnes, D., Britton, J. and Rosen, H. (1969) *Language, the Learner and the School*. Harmondsworth: Penguin.

Barnes, D. and Todd, F. (1977) *Communication and Learning in Small Groups*. London: Routledge and Kegan Paul.

Barstow, S. (1964) *Joby*. London: Michael Joseph.

Bawden, N. (1973) *Carrie's War*. London: Gollancz.

Beauvoir, S. de (1972) *Tout Compte Fait*. Paris: Editions Gallimard.

Benton, P. (1986) *Pupil, Teacher, Poem*. London: Hodder and Stoughton.

Bullock Report (1975) *A Language for Life: Report of the Committee of Enquiry*. London: HMSO.

Cassirer, E. (1944) *An Essay on Man*. New Haven: Yale University.

Chitham, E. (1982) *The Ghost in the Water*. Harmondsworth: Penguin.

Clark, E. (1983) 'The young word-maker: a case-study of innovation in the child's lexicon', in Wanner, E. and Glietman, L. R. (eds) *Language Acquisition*. Cambridge: Cambridge University Press.

Clark, M. M. (1975) 'Why remedial? Implications of using the concept of remedial education', *Remedial Education*, 11, 5–8.

Clunies-Ross, L. and Wimhurst, S. (1983) *The Right Balance: Provision for Slow Learners in Secondary Schools*. Windsor: NFER/Nelson.

Cole, K. (1981) *Gregory's Girl*. London: Allen.

Collins, J. E. (1972) 'The remedial education hoax', *Remedial Education*, 7 (3), 9–10.

Creber, P. (1979a) 'Voiceless poems: some reflections on the use and abuse of pictures in the English classroom', *Language for Learning*. 1 (2), 86–93. Exeter: Language in Education Centre. University of Exeter.

Creber, P. (1979b) 'Voiceless poems II', *Language for Learning*. 1 (3), 139–153. Exeter: Language in Education Centre. University of Exeter.

Creber, P. (1985) 'Ninety things to do with a picture' in Creber, P. (ed.) *What are Teachers for? Part 2 (Perspectives*, 20) pp. 67–75. Exeter: School of Education. University of Exeter.

Department of Education and Science (1983) *Circular 1/83* London: HMSO

Department of Education and Science (1984) *English From 5 to 16. HMI Series Curriculum Matter I.* London: HMSO.

Dunlop, F. N. (1984) *The Education of Feeling and Emotion.* London: Allen and Unwin.

Dymond, R. (1948) 'A preliminary investigation of the relations of insight and Empathy', *J Consult. Psychol.* 12, 228–33.

Englemann, J., Osborn, E. and Englemann, J. (1969) *Distar: An Instructional System.* Chicago, IL: SRA.

Frank, A. (1947) *The Diary of Anne Frank* (trans. B. M. Mooyaart-Doubleday, 1953) London: Vallentine-Mitchell.

Gordon, M. and Wilcox, S. (1983) 'Integration or alienation?', *Times Educational Supplement*, 9 September, p. 47.

Gregory, J. (1967) 'Poetry in remedial classes', *Remedial Education*, 2 (2), 33–35.

Gribble, J. (1983) *Literary Education: A Revaluation.* Cambridge: Cambridge University Press.

Gusdorf, G. (1953) *La Parole.* Paris: Presses Universitaires de France.

Hargreaves, D. H. (1976) 'Learning to be deviant in school: aspects of the hidden curriculum' in Roberts, T. (ed.) (1976) *The Circumstances of Learning*, pp. 75–97. Manchester: The University of Manchester.

Hargreaves, D. H. (1980) 'Social Class, the curriculum and the low achiever in the secondary school', *Educational Review Occasional Publications 7*, pp. 19–40.

Hargreaves, D. H. (1982) *The Challenge for the Comprehensive School.* London: Routledge and Kegan Paul.

Hargreaves Report (1984) *Improving Secondary Schools: Report of the Committee on the Curriculum and Organisation of Secondary Schools.* London: ILEA.

Harrison, B. (1983a) *English 11–18: An Arts-Based Approach.* London: Hodder and Stoughton.

Harrison, B. (1983b) *Learning Through Writing: Stages of Growth.* Windsor: NFER/Nelson.

Harrison, B. T. (1986) *Sarah's Letters: A Case of Shyness.* Bedford Way Papers 26. London: University Institute of Education.

Heaney, S. (1982) *Preoccupations.* London: Faber.

Hines, B. (1968) *A Kestrel for a Knave.* London: Michael Joseph, published as *Kes* (1969) Harmondsworth: Penguin.

Hinton, N. (1980) *Collision Course.* Harmondsworth: Penguin.

Hinton, N. (1982) *Buddy.* London: Dent.

Holbrook, D. (1964) *English for the Rejected.* Cambridge: Cambridge University Press.

Holden, E. (1906) *Nature Notes*, published as *The Country Diary of an Edwardian Lady.* (1977) London: Michael Joseph.

Holt, J. (1965) *How Children Fail.* New York: Pitman.

Hourd, M. (1951) *Some Emotional Aspects of Learning.* London: Heinemann.

Kohl, H. (1974) *Reading: How To.* Harmondsworth: Penguin.

Langer, S. (1942) *Philosophy in a New Key.* Cambridge, Mass: Harvard University Press.

Lawrence, D. (1973) *Improving Reading Through Counselling.* London: Ward Lock.

Lawrence, D. (1985) 'Improving Self-esteem and Reading', *Educational Research*, **27** (3), 194–200.

Lawrence, D. H. (1915) *The Rainbow*. London: Methuen.

Lawrence, D. H. (1921) *Women in Love*. London: Martin Secker.

Lingard, J. (1970) *Twelfth of July*. London: Hamilton.

Lomas, P. (1973) *True and False Experience*. London: Allan Lane.

Lomas, P. (1981) *The Case for a Personal Psychotherapy*. Oxford: Oxford University Press.

Lunzer, E. and Gardner, K. (eds) (1979) *The Effective Use of Reading*. London: Heinemann.

Macmurray, J. (1935) *Reason and Emotion*. London: Faber and Faber.

Meek, M. (1985) 'Play and paradoxes: some considerations of imagination and language', in Wells, G. and Nicholls, J. (eds) (1985) *Language and Learning: An Interactional Perspective*. London: Falmer.

Maslow, A. (1975) 'A Holistic Approach to Creativity', in Taylor, C. W. (ed.) (1975) *Climate for Creativity*. London: Wiley.

Milner, M. (1971) *On Not Being Able To Paint*. London: Heinemann.

Morgan, R. (1976)'"Paired-reading" tuition: a preliminary report on a technique for cases of reading deficit', *Child: Care, health, and development*, **2**, 13–28.

Morgan, R. and Lyon, E. (1979) '"Paired-reading" — a Preliminary report on a technique for tuition of reading-retarded children', *Journal of Child Psychology and Psychiatry*, **20**, 151–160.

Natale, S. (1972) *An Experiment in Empathy*. Windsor: NFER.

O'Brien, R. (1976) *Z for Zachariah*. London: Victor Gollancz.

Philpott, A. R. (1976) *Puppets and Therapy*. Parts 1–3. London: Educational Puppetry Association.

Protherough, R. (1983) *Developing Response to Fiction*. Milton Keynes: Open University Press.

Pumfrey, P. (1986) 'Paired reading: promise and pitfalls', *Educational Research*, **28** (2) 89–94.

Rogers, C. (1975) 'Empathy — an unappreciated way of being', *Counselling Psychology*, **5** (2), 2–9.

Rogers, C. (1983) *Freedom to Learn For the Eighties*. Columbus: Merrill.

Ross, M. (1978) *The Creative Arts*. London: Heinemann.

Taylor, C. W. (ed.) (1975) *Climate for Creativity*. London: Wiley.

Shelton, K. (1984) *Skill Teach*. Sheffield: Pavic Publication Sheffield City Polytechnic.

Stratta, L., Dixon, J. and Wilkinson, A. (1973) *Patterns of Language: explorations of the teaching of English*. London: Heinemann.

Swindell, R. (1984) *Brother in the Land*. Oxford: Oxford Univ. Press.

Swinson, J. (1986) 'Paired-reading: Why all the fuss?', *Special Children*, 2, 24–25.

Tate, J. (1984) *See You and Other Stories*, Harlow: Longmans.

Thornton, G. (1974) *Language, Experience and School*. London: Arnold.

Tough, J. (1973) *Focus on Meaning*. London: Unwin.

Townsend, S. (1982) *The Secret Diary of Adrian Mole*, London: Methuen.

Visser, J. (1986) 'Support: a description of the work of the S.E.N. professional', *Support Learning*, **1** (4), 5–9.

Walker, D. (1979) *Dilemmas*. Edward Arnold.

Walsh, B. (1979) 'Language Growth and Personal Growth Through Learning with Puppetry: A Teaching Approach with Case-Studies', Unpublished M.Ed Dissertation. University of Sheffield.

Walsh, B. (1983) 'The Basics and Remedial English', in Harrison, B. (ed.) (1983) *English 11–18: An arts-based approach*. London: Hodder and Stoughton.

Walsh, B. (1986) 'My language, our language: expression and communication in learning', Unpublished PhD Thesis, University of Sheffield.

Warnock, M. (1976) *Imagination*. London: Faber.

Warnock Report (1978) *Special Educational Needs: Report of the Committee of Enquiry into the education of handicapped children and young people*. London: HMSO.

Weber, K. (1974) *Yes, They Can!: A Practical Guide for Teaching the Adolescent Slow Learner*. London: Methuen.

Weber, K. (1982) *The Teacher is the Key*. Milton Keynes: Open University Press.

Weir, R. H. (1962) *Language in the Crib*. London: Mouton.

Westall, R. (1975) *The Machine Gunners*. London: Macmillan.

Wheldall, K. and Metten, P. (1985) 'Behavioural peer tutoring: Training 16-year-old tutors to employ the 'pause, prompt and praise' method with 12-year-old remedial readers', *Educational Psychology*, 5 (1), 27–44.

Wilkinson, A. (1971) *The Foundations of Language*. Oxford: Oxford University Press.

Wilkinson, A. (1985) 'I communicate — therefore I am', *Educational Review*, 37 (1), 65–77.

Wilkinson, A. (1986) *The Writing of Writing*. Milton Keynes: Open University Press.

Winnicott, D. (1958) *Collected Papers: Through Paediatrics to Psycho-analysis*. London: Tavistock.

Winnicott, D. (1971) *Playing and Reality*. London: Tavistock.

Witkin, R. (1974) *The Intelligence of Feeling*. London: Heinemann.

Name Index

Abbs, P.   2, 59
Axline, V.   86, 102

Barnes, D.   12, 80
Barnes, D.   2, 9, 12, 30, 53, 80
Benton, P.   21

Clarke, E.   8, 24
Clunies-Ross, L.   30
Creber, P.   25

Dixon, J.   4, 117
Dunlop, F. N.   3

Gordon, M.   5, 6, 53
Gregory, J.   102
Gusdorf, G.   1

Hargreaves, D. H.   1, 4
Harrison, B.   2, 65, 74
Hourd, M.   5, 117

Kohl, H.   31, 35

Lawrence, D.   34, 35
Lomas, P.   50, 114

Maslow, A.   115–16
Morgan, R.   31

Protherough, R.   45
Pumfrey, P.   31, 32

Rogers, C.   11, 34

Stratta, L.   116–17

Todd, F.   12, 80

Weber, K.   9, 10
Wilcox, S.   5, 6, 53
Wilkinson, A.   1, 117
Winnicott, D.   104, 114, 115, 116

Subject Index